IMAGES OF WALES

CILFYNYDD

To Wendy –

Very best wishes

Dean Powell

IMAGES OF WALES

CILFYNYDD

DEAN POWELL

TEMPUS

*This book is dedicated with love to Dad; my best friend and a
Llantrisant man who will always be a Cilfynydd boy*

Frontispiece: The Powell family outside their home at No. 6 Oakland Crescent, Cilfynydd, *c.* 1950.
From left to right are Steve, Sylvia, Alan and David (the author's father). The author, Dean Powell,
was born in Llantrisant and is both a Freeman and Trustee of the town. He graduated from
the University of Wales College, Swansea, with a Bachelor of Arts degree in English and Welsh,
becoming editor of the *Pontypridd & Llantrisant Observer* and literary editor of the *Western Mail.*
He currently works for BBC Wales, and is a popular guest speaker on television and radio. A life
member of Treorchy Male Choir, he is their regular compére and tenor soloist and has undertaken
a series of successful tours to Canada, America and Australia, where he performed in venues
throughout Perth, Brisbane, Melbourne, and at the Sydney Opera House. Dean is also their publicity
officer and honorary archivist and was recently presented to Her Majesty the Queen and the Duke
of Edinburgh at the Royal Variety Performance. This is his sixth book for Tempus.

First published 2006

Tempus Publishing Limited
The Mill, Brimscombe Port,
Stroud, Gloucestershire, GL5 2QG
www.tempus-publishing.com

© Dean Powell, 2006

The right of Dean Powell to be identified as the Author
of this work has been asserted in accordance with the
Copyrights, Designs and Patents Act 1988.

British Library Cataloguing in Publication Data.
A catalogue record for this book is available from the British Library.

ISBN 0 7524 3780 1

Typesetting and origination by Tempus Publishing Limited.
Printed in Great Britain.

Contents

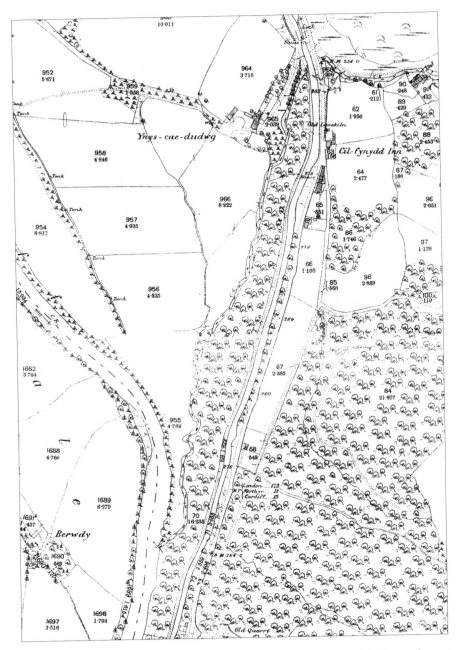

Ordnance Survey map of Cilfynydd, 1875. In 1839, only five dwellings existed in the north-west part of the parish of Eglwysilan. Pantddu, with sixty acres, was owned by Benjamin Hall MP, husband of Lady Llanover and the Commissioner for Work at the Houses of Parliament, and from whom the name Big Ben originated. It was occupied throughout the 1830s by Margaret Williams. Cwmeldeg, with 104 acres, was owned by John Llewellyn and occupied by Griffiths Davies. Cilfynydd Farm, with 211 acres, was owned by Elizabeth Morgan and occupied by David Edwards. Bodwenarth, with 137 acres, was owned by Anne Bassett and occupied by William Jenkins. Finally there was a small cottage and garden near Nant Caedudwg. All farms were owned by absentee landlords, except Pantddu where Hall retained fifty-one acres of the land to grow trees for commercial purposes.

Introduction

Cilfynydd epitomises the universal image we have of a typical Welsh mining village: born out of industrialisation, nurtured under the shadow of the colliery wheel, and the survivor of poverty and adversity with a fighting spirit. With the discovery of coal in the latter part of the nineteenth century, what was once a quiet agricultural region became transformed by those early mining pioneers who penetrated the land indiscriminately in search of their 'black gold'. The early inhabitants came from all over Wales and England and developed Cilfynydd into a cultural, spiritual, commercial and industrial centre. Those monotonous terraced streets, clinging precariously to the hillside, have become the birthplace of thousands of individuals proud to call Cilfynydd their home.

The Glamorganshire Canal, which had linked industrious Merthyr Tydfil to the docks at Cardiff since 1794, ran through Cilfynydd, then known as Ynyscaedudwg, and served as a convenient stop-off point for the barges. The Cilfynydd Inn was a popular destination for travellers, particularly during the time of the regular stagecoach service, which ran from Brecon to Cardiff. Surprisingly large quantities of material were still being transported on the Glamorganshire Canal as late as the 1860s, although it was the coming of the Taff Vale Railway which allowed for the rapid movement of the vast reserves of coal that were produced after this date. The railway line, which skirted on the opposite side of the valley to Cilfynydd, was engineered by Isambard Kingdom Brunel and opened in April 1841.

The 1839 tithe apportionment map of Eglwysilan parish shows only four farms in this north-west corner, namely Cilfynydd, Pant Ddu, Bodwenarth and Cwmeldeg and a few cottages near Nantcaedudwg. The overall population of the district of Ynyscaedudwg, named after the farm that was actually located in the parish of Llanfabon, was fewer than two dozen. Yet life in this peaceful hamlet in the Taff Valley, between the expanding Pontypridd and neighbouring mining village of Abercynon, changed forever with the emergence of the Albion Steam Coal Co.

The search for coal began on the site of Ynyscaedudwg Farm in December 1884 and was completed by August 1887, when the first saleable fuel was raised. There seemed to be little doubt in the minds of the company directors that rich reserves would be found there because houses for colliery workers were built before the first dram load reached the surface. Their confidence was well founded, and by 1891 the population numbered well over 3,000. The majority of the housing and public buildings date from the period of fastest industrial growth – between 1885 and 1910 – by which time eleven terraces of houses ran in parallel lines roughly north to south along the hillside.

A branch of the Taff Vale Railway was constructed which left the main line at the northern end of Berw Road, Pontypridd, crossed the river Taff over a new iron viaduct, built in 1885, and then ran alongside the Glamorganshire Canal to the Albion Colliery. Passenger traffic began in June 1900 when Cilfynydd obtained its own station and the village was to officially receive its new name. At one point it seemed likely that Albion Town would be adopted, but following public opposition, residents settled on the name of one of the farms, Cilfynydd, meaning mountain hollow or retreat. The postal authorities accepted the outcome of a public meeting and the village of Cilfynydd was officially recognised.

By this time, six Nonconformist chapels, largely Welsh speaking, named Rehoboth, Bethel, Beulah, Moriah, Primitive Methodist and Bethany, along with St Luke's church, were established to minister to the spiritual needs of the population. There were four public houses, and Richard Street had become the hub of local commerce. Two thirds of Cilfynydd farmland disappeared as the new village grew and the colliery spoil heap behind Mary Street rapidly increased in equal measure.

The first school was opened in the vestry of Moriah Welsh Congregational Chapel in Ann Street. So many families had moved into the area that ninety-four children were enrolled at this temporary accommodation in the first week. By November 1887, the education board agreed to purchase an acre of land for £475 on which a school could be built, and within a few short years the register increased to a staggering 996 pupils. The new school opened in April 1889 with a building each for the boys, girls and infants, and the first headmaster, Richard Williams, remained in the post for almost forty years.

Cilfynydd continued to flourish, but in June 1894 tragedy struck. After only seven years of productive life, a horrific explosion occurred in the Albion Colliery on Saturday 23 June. The results were appalling, causing the death of 290 men and boys and making it the worst colliery disaster in mining history at that time. The tragedy naturally had a profound effect on the lives of every individual in the village, but with remarkable endurance and fighting spirit they overcame the horror. Yet further devastation was not far away when, in 1913, a tornado of Biblical proportions struck the village.

Throughout both world wars, gallant young men from Cilfynydd fought bravely for king and country. The village also began to grow still further with added housing developments on the mountain to the south. Despite the years of economic depression, commercially, spiritually and culturally Cilfynydd had fulfilled its potential. The village enjoyed a reputation as a breeding ground for first-class sportsmen, boasting successful boxers, rugby and football players. Cilfynydd Rugby Football Club enjoyed an enviable reputation throughout Wales. Culturally and academically, Cilfynydd's output of gifted figures has been incredible. William Street boasts the birthplace of a Welsh rugby international, a leading politician and two of the world's greatest opera singers. From other parts of the village came a famous composer and a popular singer with the country's leading orchestra.

The closure of the Albion Colliery in 1966 left the village without its main source of employment, and gradually it became a village in decline. The very essence of Cilfynydd, the reason behind its very origin, was gone forever. So too were many of its landmark buildings, with the subsequent closure of many chapels, the Workmen's Hall, Richard's Hotel, Albion Hotel and the majority of stores throughout its long terraced streets. Yet despite such an often agonizing, tumultuous history, Cilfynydd remains a remarkable Welsh village and one that so many are proud to still call their home.

Dean Powell
January 2006

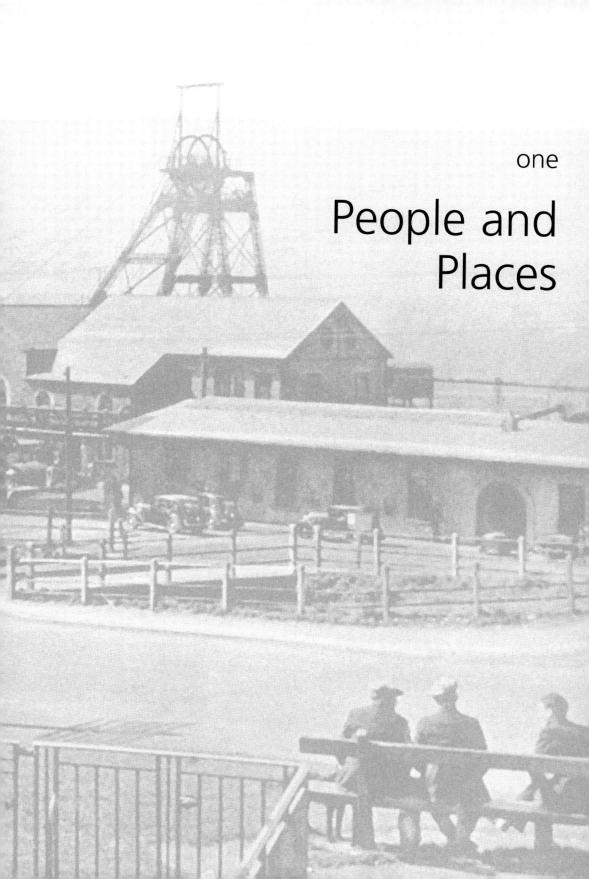

one

People and
Places

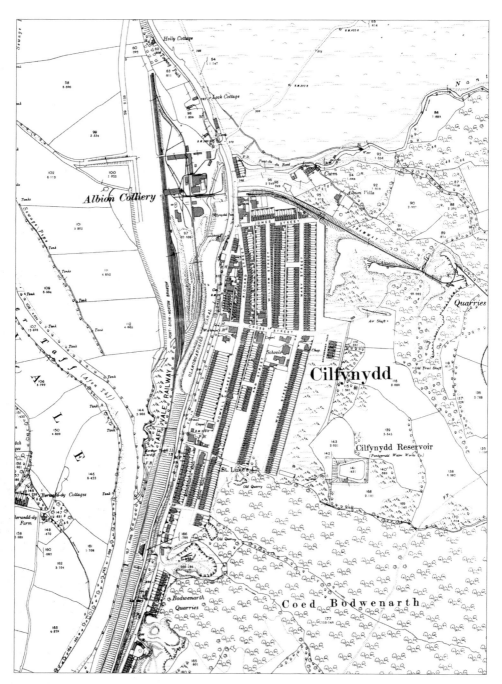

Ordnance Survey map of Cilfynydd, 1900. The scene has changed dramatically in comparison with the previous map. Nine terraces of houses have been built, along with six chapels, three public houses, a school, church, post office, Workmen's Hall and the Albion Colliery. Notice there is no Oakland Terrace or Crescent; these were built in 1905 and 1936 respectively, and the housing estates further along the mountainside appeared after 1950.

View of the north end of Cilfynydd, taken from the bus terminus, 1977. Also in view is Eglwysilan Mountain and Bodwenarth Wood. The land to the north of Nantcaedudwg became known as Cilfynydd Common, though its official title on the old Ordnance Survey maps is Graig Evan Leyshon. During the First World War, an Act of Parliament dated 1916 gave the right to create allotments on the common land.

Cilfynydd Road, looking north towards Abercynon. The Cilfynydd Inn is on the right, with the Albion Colliery on the left. Note the overhead power cables for the trolleybuses, which began at John Street, Treforest, and ended at the bus terminus. Sprawled across Graig Evan Leyshon Common is the Abercynon Colliery coal tip. Immediately behind the railings on the left was the Glamorganshire Canal.

Cilfynydd, 1906. Rehoboth Baptist Chapel is to the left of centre with Bethel Methodist Chapel immediately behind. In the centre is Moriah Welsh Congregational Chapel, with the Workmen's Hall in front. The Commercial Hotel (known as The Spite) stands in front, and to the right of the hall is Dundella House, the village surgery and home of Dr Tudor Williams. The empty coal trucks can be seen on the left, waiting to move into the sidings to be loaded. The Albion Steam Coal Co. owned over 600 coal trucks and the sidings could hold more than 700.

Cwmeldeg, *c.* 1910. The large house in the trees is Albion House, the pit manager's residence. In the centre are the Cwm Cottages, long since demolished. The leet is the channel that carried water from Nantcaedudwg to the Glamorganshire Canal to top up its water level when needed. It was affectionately known as The Feeder. Its remains can still be seen in places, especially near the War Memorial. The building to the bottom right was the slaughterhouse owned by the Evans family of Richard Street. Children often called here for animal bladders to use as footballs.

Graig Evan Leyshon Cottages and the spoil heap from Abercynon Colliery, with the overhead lines which carried the buckets containing spoil. During the depression years men picked coal on the side of the tip, a very risky procedure, especially when the buckets were upturned. A small stone building stood in isolation in the middle of the common which held the explosives used in the Albion Colliery. In 1941, a stray bomb from a German aircraft narrowly missed the store. About halfway along the old parish road to Llanfabon were Cwmeldeg cottages. Above the cottages was Cwmeldeg Uchaf Farm, with Cwmeldeg Isaf Farm below. The living room of the cottage closest to Cilfynydd was used as a polling booth for elections and was officially recognised as the smallest polling station in Britain. The cottages were demolished in the 1970s.

Cilfynydd Road. When the Albion Colliery opened, the area was rapidly built up with parallel rows of houses, shops, chapels, church, pubs and a school. The stone came from pennant sandstone quarries south of the village behind Brynderwen Road. Bricks were made locally and slates were brought from North Wales to Cardiff before being transported along the Glamorganshire Canal.

The Cilfynydd Inn was built in the early nineteenth century. Its first licensees were Enoch and Mary Thomas. It was located opposite the Glamorganshire Canal and alongside the main road running north to south through the Taff Valley. Originally built with stable accommodation where coaching or canal horses could be housed, the inn lay roughly halfway between Merthyr and Cardiff and it would certainly have been a convenient stopping point for travellers. The stables were later converted into a skittle alley. When the Albion Colliery was sunk in 1884 the inn served as a hostel for some of the sinkers.

The Square, *c.* 1931. On the left is the Cilfynydd Inn. Further along Cilfynydd Road is a trolleybus close to the police station (built in 1901) and the Richards Hotel. The tramway service in the village began on 6 March 1905 and ran from Cilfynydd through Pontypridd to Treforest. It continued for twenty-five years until it was replaced on 18 September 1930 by the trolleybuses. Two of the most memorable bus conductors were Brinley Jones and Olive Hunt.

Commercial Hotel, 1967. This public house is more commonly known as The Spite. The Richards Hotel was built shortly after the sinking of the colliery, and it is believed that a rival brewery opened the Commercial Hotel further along the road at the same time to 'spite' them. Hence the establishment's nickname.

Albion Hotel on Cilfynydd Road, 1886, photographed prior to the building of Howell Street at the rear. Thomas William was landlord of the hotel in 1894, followed in 1897 by William Rees. Fred Warren took over during the First World War, followed by Tom Jones in 1926. From the 1940s onwards, the licensee was David Ebenezer and after he died his wife and daughters, Tegwen and Megan, ran the establishment.

Cilfynydd Road, looking south toward Pontsionnorton, *c.* 1890. The mystery as to why Cilfynydd Road commences at No. 5, near the War Memorial, is solved here. Numbers one to four are on the right of the picture, at the south end of the village, prior to being demolished. Few are sure where the village's street names originated. Some suggest that the manager of the Albion Colliery, William Jones, had children named Richard, Ann, Mary, William and Howell. Others believe they are the names of the children of John Rosser of Bodwenarth Quarry, from where the stone came to build the streets themselves.

Colliery Sidings, looking towards the first houses being built in Glyncoch, *c.* 1950. Note the rounded capped hill in the background, known as the bald-headed mountain. Parallel to Cilfynydd Road, close to where the Cilfynydd Inn now stands, was a two-acre field known as Cae y Gof (The Blacksmith's Field), but no record of a blacksmith's shop can be traced.

Cilfynydd Road, near King's Garage, *c.* 1930. Cilfynydd Road formed part of the route from Merthyr to Cardiff, and was built in the late 1760s at the instigation of Anthony Bacon, one of the first ironmasters of Merthyr Tydfil. Later, in 1794, came the Glamorganshire Canal, parallel on the western side of the road, with most of those working on the canal living in Pontsionnorton and Newbridge (renamed Pontypridd in 1856).

Opposite below: The Albion Hotel on Cilfynydd Road, 1967. The inn was one of several businesses in the village to close due to the economic decline which came following the closure of the Albion Colliery. The hotel, then run by Mr Parsons, was also prone to severe flooding.

Repair work being carried out on the Glamorganshire Canal. Although the canal could no longer be used beyond the landslide, it was still operating as far as Pontypridd. Subsequently, a water supply was needed, and as that could only come from The Feeder from Nantcaedudwg it was necessary to build a wooden trough to convey the water over the gap which was never filled. The landslide blocked the railway lines to the Albion Colliery and Nelson. The section between Abercynon and Cilfynydd was closed in 1915 and the remaining section between Pontypridd and Cardiff closed in 1942. The whole canal was abandoned in January 1944.

Lincoln Potato Stores on Cilfynydd Road, pictured before the building of Bedw Terrace. Notice the tramlines on the road, the overhead power cables and the trucks bringing stone from the quarry. The Glamorganshire Canal opposite skirted the village on its western side, eventually arriving at Bodwenarth Quarries. Here, too, canal horses could be shod at the blacksmith's shop. Bodwenarth Terrace was known as 'Bucket Street' because, before the building of Bedw Terrace, coal was dumped on Cilfynydd Road and carried to the houses above in buckets.

King's Garage in the 1950s. Gerald King arrived from Ireland during a motor industry strike in the early 1920s and worked at various places in the valleys, but chiefly as a mechanic and driver for the Cynon Star Motors in Abercynon. He drove their famous open-topped charabanc, the Cynon Star. His family had been landowners who lost their land and fortune in the latter part of the nineteenth century. He was connected by marriage to Lord and Lady Massey of Killay Castle, County Tipperary. After leaving the Cynon Star Motors he bought a blacksmith's shop on Cilfynydd Road to start his own business, becoming one of the many pioneers in the charabanc business in the valleys.

A view of Cilfynydd from the spoil tip, with Albion House centre right, c. 1970. The spoil from the colliery was conveyed by drams from the colliery yard on a narrow-gauge railway that went under the canal and road midway between the Cilfynydd Inn and Park Place, then behind Jones Street before beginning the steep ascent. Until 1919, tipping took place behind Mary Street. An engine house was built at the top of the mountain beyond the existing quarries and the spoil was tipped to the side and behind Cilfynydd Farm. The steel rope occasionally snapped, allowing the dram to run free before crashing into the gardens of Jones Street. Riding on the drams was illegal but was often too tempting for young boys.

Cilfynydd War Memorial, with the 'tin shed' on the left and the Albion Colliery, *c.* 1950. The war memorial was unveiled by Brigadier General the Hon. C.G. Bruce on Thursday 29 October 1925. A procession, led by the Treforest Silver Band, proceeded from the Workmen's Hall to the memorial, which was dedicated by the Lord Bishop of Llandaff. Alongside the 'tin shed' was a cabin on wheels used by the local branch of the South Wales Miners' Federation. The large structure (centre) was the cooling tower for the steam boilers. During repair work on the stack (left) a workman fell to his death inside. The road bridge crossed the canal and was built in 1922.

The bridge over Nantcaedudwg, alongside the Cwm Cottages. The stream was used to wash clothes. During the 1960s, some villagers from Cwmeldeg claimed to have seen the ghost of the 'White Lady' haunting the wooded slopes. Older residents claimed that, prior to the Albion Colliery Disaster, she was seen riding a white horse through Wood Street and Mary Street. One night in the 1960s a crowd of several hundred villagers climbed the mountain side in hope of sighting the apparition.

The Cwm, or Cil Baths, below Cwmeldeg. It was built by the Albion Steam Coal Co. to supply water to the colliery. Of course, it was a popular bathing area for the villagers and often used for swimming competitions, becoming a very popular spot during the summer months.

Gwenllian Llywellyn (1859-1948). Born at Cwmeldeg Farm, Gwenllian's mother, grandmother and their maidservant all died of typhoid when she was twelve. The remainder of the family moved to St Mellons, but when her father died four years later Gwenllian was sent to her aunt at Llanharan, where she met Dr William Price, the famed surgeon, chartist, arch Druid and pioneer of cremation. Recognising her as his 'goddess', they were married in a Druidic ceremony at Pontypridd's Rocking Stone on William's eighty-first birthday in March 1881. Gwenllian was just twenty-two. They lived in Ty'r Clettwr, Llantrisant, and in 1883 she gave birth to a son, named Iesu Grist (Jesus Christ). Five months later the baby died and the doctor famously cremated him on a mountain top. A crown court case followed; Gwenllian was the subject of intense police questioning. Price defended himself brilliantly before the judge and jury, resulting in his acquittal. The case led to the passing of the Cremation Act in 1902. Gwenllian and William had two further children, named Iesu Grist II (renamed Nicholas) and Penelopen. Dr Price died in 1893, aged ninety-three, as he sipped champagne with Gwenllian by his side. She later married John Parry, and they had a daughter together named Rachel.

Cilfynydd railway station and Burgess Bakery delivery vans. When the Albion Colliery opened in 1887, Cilfynydd was isolated from the Taff Vale Railway, which ran on the opposite side of the Taff Valley. To get around this problem a branch line was constructed which left the main line at the end of Berw Road, crossed the river Taff over a new iron viaduct built in 1884, and ran alongside the Glamorganshire Canal to the Albion. The line was later extended north and linked with the Nelson branch. Passenger traffic began in June 1900 when Cilfynydd obtained its own station. The line closed to passenger traffic on 12 September 1932, but was used for school excursions until 1936.

Burgess Bakery staff, pictured outside their premises. Father and son, Henry and Harry Burgess, are pictured in the front, while standing second left is Trevor Butler, who later became manager of the bakery. The firm, situated behind the Cilfynydd Inn, was a very successful enterprise, supplying bread to Pontypridd and its surrounding villages.

Cilfynydd Welfare Ground, *c.* 1930. The area was situated below the Albion Colliery. It was always a popular location, with tennis courts, a bowling green, rugby ground and children's playground, maintained for many years under the watchful eye of Mr Hennessey. Note the 'top' tip in the centre of the skyline.

A view towards the Unemployed Hall, Burgess Bakery, Park Place and the rear of Cilfynydd Road (or Queen's Square), around the 1950s. In the foreground is the road to the Cwm and a rather dry bed of Nantcaedudwg. Glyncoch is also beginning to grow in the distance. The Unemployed Hall is an example of the buildings erected between the two world wars as a result of the low employment rate. It was used by groups like St John's Ambulance, and later became the village scout hall.

Cilfynydd Square, Richard Street, early 1900s. On the left-hand side of Richard Street can be seen a barber's pole. This shop was once occupied by D.S. Williams, barber.

Richard Street, c. 1910. The commercial centre of the village enjoyed a vast array of businesses, including Henry Bennett (boot dealer), Margaret Morris (draper), Henry Burgess (confectioner) and Michael Cohen (painter). There was also Price & Sons (boot makers) and Caroline Cridland (clothier). Further along was Thomas Pugh the draper and David Davies' shop for groceries and boots. Benjamin Rosser had a butcher's shop and Edward Edwards was a tailor and hatter.

Evans' butchers on Richard Street was opened in 1887 by Charles Evans, one of twenty-one children from Aberystwyth. A staunch member of Bethel Methodist Chapel, he also owned the slaughterhouse near the Cwm Cottages. The shop remained in the family for the next 112 years. He was succeeded by his son, David Charles Evans, followed by his son, David Lynn Evans, and finally his son, Charles Stuart Evans, who ran it from 1983. The shop eventually closed in 1999. It was the oldest established family business in the village.

Richard Street, c. 1920. Some of the many shopkeepers on the street at this time included Evan Evans (tailor), John Simmonds (butcher), Thomas Evans (draper), Gwilym Thomas (grocer), William Games (builder), John Thomas (grocer) and John Hopkins (watchmaker). Further along the street was George Howells (flannel dealer), Charles James (tailor), William Jenkins (grocer), John David Jones (draper), Margaret Jones (grocer), Knight & Sons (butchers), Stephen Lewis (newsagent), Thomas Ivor Lewis (barber), Evan Morgan (the Hong Kong Grocery), Charles Evans (butcher) and Albert Edward Moore (hairdresser and ales).

Harry Morgan (1910-87). Harry was born in Trallwn in 1910, the son of Peter Samuel and Harriet Elizabeth Morgan. He learned his trade as a barber at Maison Samuel Hairdressing Salon in Taff Street, Pontypridd, as well as serving in the RAF between 1941 and 1944. In 1937 he opened his hairdressing business at No. 5 Richard Street, moving to No. 19 a few years later. Harry was a keen Cardiff City supporter and was actively involved in the local amateur dramatic society in Cilfynydd. He eventually retired in 1967 and died in 1987.

Opposite above: Unemployed miners in Richard Street during the year-long Cambrian Colliery dispute of 1911. They are awaiting admittance to the Workmen's Hall to hold a protest meeting.

Seymour & Sons was one of the oldest establishments in the village, selling everything from fresh fruit to paraffin. The last member of the family, Charles Seymour, still served in the shop for many years after the Second World War

Albion Supper Bar at the bottom of Richard Street, *c.* 1905. One of the many popular cafés in the district, it was often the centre for local gossip in this close-knit community.

Ken Davies behind the counter of his shop, Bon Ton, in Richard Street. He originally ran a similar shop near the Fountain, Pontypridd. As can be seen by the quantity of hat boxes on the shelves behind him, Mr Davies ran a popular milliner's business in the village.

Richard Street, *c*. 1955. At No. 3 was John Bennett, the cobbler, with Harry Morgan's barber shop at No. 5, before he moved further along Richard Street. The old bench can be seen near the cottages. It was a favourite spot for the elderly men of the village to meet and put the world to rights!

John Bennett with his sister-in-law, Lil, outside his cobbler's shop at No. 3 Richard Street in July 1954. The aroma of leather, polish and dyes is a nostalgic memory for those who still recall the shop.

Antonio (Tony) Carini (1919-67). One of two children, his parents, Francesco (who died when the *Arandora Star* was sunk) and Angela Carini, moved to South Wales from the Bardi region of Italy. As with so many other Italian families in the valleys, they opened a café. The first Carini's Café was situated at the bottom of Richard Street, before moving to new premises further along the street some years later. Tony later took over the business and his wife, Maria, whom he married in 1952, continued running it after his death until 1976. The café was a favourite meeting place, the backroom usually warmed by an open fire. Tony also ran a successful ice-cream business in the village, taking his cart to the Cwm Baths on hot summer days. A popular scout leader, he was also a keen photographer.

Richard Street, with the Cilfynydd Inn on the right-hand side. Six licensed premises have operated in the village at various times, namely: the Cilfynydd RFC Clubhouse, Cilfynydd Inn, Richards Hotel, Commercial Hotel, Albion Hotel and the Cilfynydd Constitutional Club, which opened in 1890. The house to the left of centre was owned by Mr Osbourne, who spent most of his leisure time sitting on the low wall outside.

Cottages along Cilfynydd Road, at the foot of Richard's Street. At one time they enjoyed the luxury of front gardens, but these were removed with the widening of the busy road outside.

Owen Hughes, from Ann Street, was a descendant of the well-known Penwern family. A miner at the Albion Colliery, Mr Hughes fractured his spine during a roof collapse at the pit in 1945, which left him a paraplegic. He underwent extensive treatment at Rookwood Hospital in Cardiff. Despite his injuries, he mastered the arts of archery and bowls and entered the Paraplegic Olympics in Australia and the Commonwealth Games in Jamaica during the 1960s, winning a silver medal for archery. He is pictured in his second specially adapted invalid car. Mr Hughes, who was married to Lilly and had a daughter, Gillian, died in 1974.

Richard Street, *c.* 1950. At one time, one of the oldest paper boys working for Brown's newsagent on Richard Street was Johnny Combes, a retired miner, who was still delivering newspapers throughout the village at the age of seventy-five.

Howell Street leading to Richard Street, with Cross Street cutting through the middle. The Workmen's Hall is on left. Howell Street is home to St Luke's church, but also once included the British Legion Hall (formerly the Wesleyan Welsh Chapel), Atkinson's store and the Ynysybwl Co-operative Society. The street is divided into two, with Bedw Terrace to the south eventually going downhill to connect with Bodwenarth Terrace and Cilfynydd Road.

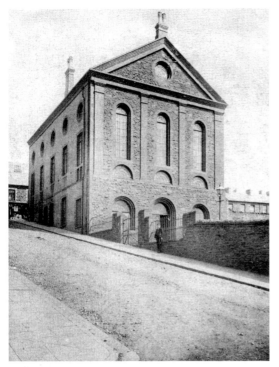

Cilfynydd Workmen's Hall was built by subscription from miners at the Albion Colliery. As with the village's church and chapels, the Workmen's Hall served as an important meeting place and social centre. A drama was performed there every week during the 1950s, when you might see six of the best companies in South Wales, coming from such places as Aberdare, Blackwood, Cardiff, Bridgend and Treharris. The hall also contained reading rooms and a library on the ground floor. It was a successful auditorium for stage performances and later became a popular bingo hall.

Cilfynydd Workmen's Hall Committee. From left to right, back row: Gomer Harris, -?-, Mr Jones, Rhys (Penwern) Williams, Richard Jones, ? Morgan, Ron Cox, -?-, -?-. Front row: -?-, -?-, Vince Griffiths, Emrys Peck, ? Jones, Harry Williams, ? Thomas and ? Jenkins. Emrys Peck devoted much of his life to public service as a local councillor, and was later made chairman of the Mid Glamorgan County Council.

Dr Tudor Williams JP. Born in Carmarthen, Dr Williams began his career as a pharmacist, before training at the Royal Middlesex Hospital to become a qualified doctor in 1913. Seven years later he came to Cilfynydd as the general practitioner. His brother, David, was the local GP for Taff's Well. Dr Williams and his wife, Florence, and two daughters, Jean (later Dr Jean Williams) and Phoebe (later a nursing sister), settled into the imposing Dundella House on Cilfynydd Road. This impressive building of seventeen rooms included the surgery, consultation room, dispensary and living quarters. For forty years Dr Williams served the community as both GP and leader of the St John's Ambulance Brigade, and he was also a fervent sports supporter. While so many other young doctors came to villages such as Cilfynydd before moving on to greater things, Dr Williams remained faithful to its people. In March 1965, the village turned out to show their gratitude at his retirement party in the Workmen's Hall. His daughter, Phoebe, married Dr Arthur Emmanuel who continued his father-in-law's work as the GP for Cilfynydd.

Mary Morgan, of Cilfynydd Road. A prominent figure in the village for many years, Mrs Morgan was a nurse and midwife whose skills ensured the safe delivery of the newborn. In spite of her commitment to her profession, she and her husband, Dewi, found time to have two boys of their own. The elder, Howard, was a fine cricketer, a pilot officer during the Second World War and a headteacher. His brother, Graham, participated in the D-Day landings.

H. Atkinson, butchers in Howell Street, 1922. Harry Atkinson is pictured in the doorway with his staff.

Children from Howell Street pictured during the 1926 National Strike. Although there is an air of poverty about this photograph, some children still manage to smile.

Children from Howell Street, pictured during the early 1930s. The street was once home to boxer Glen Moody – younger brother of Frank – and his family. Glen's first fight was an exhibition bout held to raise money to feed hungry children during the miners' strike of 1926. He later became Welsh middleweight and light heavyweight champion.

Some of the houses on Howell Street, and the alleyway which separated the south end of the street from Bedw Terrace. It led to Ann Street (out of sight on the left) and continued to join Wood Street and Oakland Terrace. It was prone to flooding, as can be seen by the stone and mud.

Bedw Terrace leading towards Howell Street, with the rear of Bodwenarth Terrace (Church Street) on the left. The spoil heap from Abercynon Colliery is clearly visible. Just beyond the cross on St Luke's church can be seen the section of the tip which in December 1939 slipped and blocked the main A470 road, destroying a section of the disused canal and diverting the course of the river Taff.

Four generations of the Evans family from William Street. Pictured is a young Geraint Llewellyn Evans, later Sir Geraint Evans, with his father, grandfather and great-grandfather. In 1992, Geraint said: 'In William Street doors were never locked, and people helped each other in times of distress. If anybody was taken ill, there would always be a voice at the door, offering to do their washing. Life was warm and friendly. I was raised and played with friends such as Haydn Harrison and Billy John, Ieuan Jones, Gareth Owen, Bryn Walters and Alun, my cousin who died in the war. But the most important thing for me was to marry the girl from No. 78.'

Far left: Stuart Burrows and his son, Mark, during a visit to William Street, November 1977, prior to a concert in Moriah Welsh Congregational Chapel where they both performed. A lord, a singing knight, an opera giant and a Welsh rugby international have one thing in common – they all came from William Street. Lord Merlyn Rees (No. 21), Sir Geraint Evans (No. 23), Stuart Burrows (No. 19) and Glyn Davies (No. 78) were all raised in this quiet, unassuming row of terraced houses.

Above right: Lord Merlyn Rees (1920-2006). Born in William Street, Cilfynydd on 18 December, his official title was Baron Merlyn Rees of Morely and South Leeds in the County of West Yorkshire and of Cilfynydd in the County of Mid Glamorgan. He was educated at Pontypridd Boys' Grammar School and Wembley, Middlesex, Harrow Weald Grammar School, the London School of Economics, London and Nottingham Universities.

His political propensities first became apparent at Harrow Weald. He was also good at acting, was in the first team at every sport, and had an excellent singing voice. In 1935, he stood as Labour candidate in the school's mock election. His education was interrupted by war service in the RAF between 1941 and 1946. He was a ground controller of forward units during the invasions of Sicily, Salerno, Anzio and the south of France, ending his time in the RAF as squadron leader at the age of twenty-five. He spent eleven years teaching at his old grammar school – where he met his wife Colleen – and was active in Labour circles, entering Parliament at a by-election in 1963 in the Leeds South seat, which became vacant by the death of Hugh Gaitskell. He spent the majority of his thirty years in the House of Commons on the front bench, either in government or opposition, and his decision in the early 1980s not to seek re-election onto the shadow cabinet made him one of the most experienced and seasoned back-benchers on either side of the House. His earliest mentor in the Commons was James Callaghan, who picked him as parliamentary private secretary when he was Chancellor. Then, after four unspectacular years as Defence undersecretary, Rees rejoined Callaghan at the Home Office in 1968 as race relations minister. There he acquired a reputation as an inflexible minister, keeping down immigration, invariably sustaining the decision of Home Office officials, even though the Act allowed him discretion to intervene on humanitarian grounds.

In opposition in 1970, he became Callaghan's number two as home affairs spokesman. Two years later, after working on formulating Labour's policy on Ireland, he was elected to the shadow cabinet. He was therefore already well briefed when he became Northern Ireland Secretary in 1974. The mutual dislike between Rees and Dr Ian Paisley, the Democratic Unionist leader, reached a climax in 1975 when Rees stormed out of a meeting with him and locked the door on him, after Paisley accused him of cooking up a deal with the IRA. At the Home Office, Rees took an unexpectedly hard line over crime. His experience at the Northern Ireland Office made him particularly keen on security, and he implemented several initiatives to give MPs and ministers more protection. After the Tories regained power, Rees became Shadow Home Secretary, followed by a period as Shadow Energy Secretary. He remained loyal to Neil Kinnock and was a leading figure in trying to reform Labour's constitution in the wake of the 1979 and subsequent general election defeats. After his decision not to seek re-election to the shadow cabinet, Rees became active in the campaign to prosecute alleged Nazi war criminals living in Britain. He did not fight the 1992 general election in his seat. He was made a life peer in the subsequent dissolution honours.

Lord Merlyn-Rees continued to be active in the House of Lords right into his eighties, despite having developed Parkinson's disease. He died on 5 January 2006.

Dr Gareth Owen. Born in the fish shop in Jones Street, he was educated at Pontypridd Boys' Grammar School and entered the University College of Cardiff for a year before joining the RAF during the Second World War. As a flight lieutenant, he served in both Europe and South East Asia, returning to Cardiff in 1947 to complete his studies in zoology, graduating with first-class honours in 1950. In 1953 he became a lecturer at Glasgow University before becoming Professor of Zoology at Queen's University, Belfast, between 1964 and 1979. He took up the post of pro-vice chancellor at the University of Aberystwyth between 1974 and 1979, later becoming principal between 1979 and 1989. He was later made vice-chancellor of the University of Wales between 1985 and 1987 and was awarded the CBE in the Queen's Honours List in 1988, also being made a fellow of the University of Cardiff, and an honorary member of the Gorsedd y Beirdd. He died after a short illness on 4 May 2002.

A milk delivery by horse and cart, owned by the Evans Brothers of the Celtic Dairy, outside Moriah Welsh Congregational Chapel, c. 1910.

Ann Street in 1909, with Cilfynydd School on the left. Mrs Gittins lived in the last house on the right. She had been a nurse in France during the First World War and had sadly been permanently affected by the shelling. Between the two wars she was a familiar figure around the village streets, selling toffee apples from a tray which she carried.

The top end of Ann Street, pictured when the road was in the process of being surfaced in the 1960s. Before then it was a rough track, only the bottom half being properly surfaced.

The Bennett family from Mary Street, *c.* 1900. The family settled in Cilfynydd from Llanidloes in 1885. Pictured in the centre is Mary Bennett, the village dressmaker and midwife. In the top right-hand corner is a picture of Edward Bennett, who was killed in the Albion Colliery disaster in 1894.

Cross Street, 1968. On the left in the picture can be seen a shop sign. This was the last house at the Cross Street end of William Street. It was known as Jonathan's, after a former owner. On the opposite side of the street was another general store owned by the Angwin family. Above the school was a local grocery shop owned by Mr Thomas in the 1950s, kept for many years by the Roberts family. At that time the bakehouse building (seen at the bottom right) was adjoining the road. Locals used it at Christmas to have their poultry cooked if they were lucky enough to afford such a luxury.

Cross Street to Brynderwen Terrace, 1966. High above the street loomed the coal tips, towering menacingly over the village. In October 1966, shortly after the Albion Colliery had ceased production, the Aberfan disaster occurred, when a coal tip tragically engulfed a school full of children, causing over a hundred deaths. Only a few miles away, the residents of Cilfynydd feared the same fate from the tip which dominated the skyline of their village. A two-phased scheme to reduce the steep gradient of the colliery spoil began in 1974 and was completed two years later.

Oakland Terrace, c. 1910. More than a decade after most of the streets of the village had been constructed, additional housing was needed. Oakland Terrace was built between 1906 and 1909, leading from Wood Street. The price of each house was then around £120, a small fortune in those days and the reason why so many professionals occupied the houses. The absence of traffic made it ideal for children, who have managed to make a 'bogey' out of an old pram chassis to free-wheel from the top to the bottom of the hill.

The Powell family, pictured outside their home in Oakland Crescent, *c.* 1956. On the doorstep stands Alan, who, in 1936, was the first baby born in the new Oakland Crescent. Also pictured is the author's father, David (riding his bike), Tom Powell, May Powell, Steve Powell, Barbara Powell and Mrs Morgan.

Heol y Nant and the council housing estate, built in the 1950s, behind Oakland Terrace. This picture, taken in 1967, also shows the coal tips dominating the skyline. Notice no snow has settled on the top of the slag heap because the tip itself was still burning as a result of spontaneous combustion.

Cilfynydd Reservoir, pictured in 1966. The reservoir and purifying plant served clean drinking water to the village below when required. It was built around 1920 and was connected to the Taff Fechan system.

Cilfynydd Farm, which gave the village its name. It was built during the mid-seventeenth century in the traditional 'long house' style – in which people and their animals lived in separate parts of the same building. Its 211 acres included around eighteen acres of arable land. Well over a hundred acres were in pasture and meadow on which livestock could be grazed. A large tract of land, over fifty acres, was still covered by native woodland. The tithe payable on this land for 1839 was £6 6s, of which the vicar's share was £1 13s.

Some of the Albion Colliery horses. Pictured from left to right are Mr Cummings, Mr Owen (the colliery farrier) and Mr Spear. The pit ponies that worked underground in the Albion were brought up for two weeks in the summer months to enjoy the green fields of Cilfynydd Farm.

Miners walking to work at the Albion Colliery, *c.* 1910. As far back as 1870 three trial borings were made to search for coal on Cilfynydd Farm land, in the region of Heol Nant. Coal companies were concerned largely with the Rhondda, but didn't lose sight of the land between Pontypridd and Treharris which had yet to be exploited.

Albion Colliery, *c*. 1910. In December 1884, sinking commenced on the site of Ynyscaedudwg Farm. The directors of the Albion Steam Coal Co. were sure that rich coal seams could be found in the vicinity. In August 1887 the first coal was raised, after which the village rapidly grew to house around 3,000 people.

Albion Colliery, 1900. The Glamorganshire Canal, with its towpath, can be seen on the left. The humpbacked bridge, the only access to the colliery at that time, is on the right. The two shafts, 19ft in diameter, were sunk 33 yards apart to a depth of 646 yards. During the sinking six men were killed in two separate accidents. On 24 March 1886, Richard Jones, aged twenty, and Joseph Jones, aged twenty-four, were killed by a fall of fireclay. Later that year, Thomas Jones, David Griffiths, Evan Williams and Morris Jones were killed by a collapse of brickwork lining the shaft. When in full production the average weekly output was 12,000 tons, which was the largest tonnage for a single shift coal-winding colliery in South Wales.

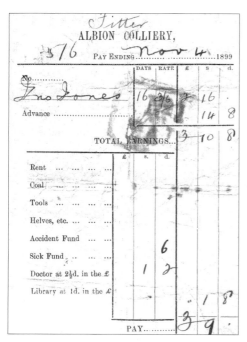

An Albion Colliery wage slip from November 1899 belonging to a fitter named Jones. The village had its own 'health system' in 1899 as can be seen by the deductions in this pay docket. It was one of the first villages in the South Wales mining area to adopt such a scheme. By 1908 the workforce had grown to 2,589 men, with 1,778 employed there by 1918. According to a report dated 1923, there were 2,334 men employed.

A photograph of Albion Colliery officials taken to commemorate Queen Victoria's Diamond Jubilee in 1897, with manager William Jones seated in the centre. The workforce came from all over the UK. The pay was relatively good compared to farming, hence many workers came from rural areas. At the enquiry into the causes of the 1894 disaster it emerged that many of the rules of the Mines Regulation Act of 1887 had been blatantly ignored. For further information see *One Saturday Afternoon* (National Museum of Wales) by Meurig Evans.

Surface workers at the Albion Colliery, *c.* 1897. Only three years earlier the village had been devastated by the worst mining disaster in British history at that time. A second explosion occurred at 3.10 p.m. on 10 November 1906 while men were carrying out repair work, probably due to the emission of sparks from an electric battery. Henry Hill, the overman, was sent underground to investigate. He found five badly burned workmen, three of whom were already dead and two who died in their homes during the next forty-eight hours. Hill continued his search but went missing. The rescue party later found his body – he had died from the effects of after-damp.

A group of Albion Colliery miners, *c.* 1905. Pictured is John Rosser (front row wearing a white scarf), a contractor, who died in October 1907 of pleurisy. He was married to Ann Morgan of Pantddu Farm, Cilfynydd, and represented the Cilfynydd Ward on the Pontypridd Burial Board.

Colliers waiting for their pay at the Albion Colliery. Pictured third from the left is miner Fatty Osbourne of Jones Street, a large gentleman who Sir Geraint Evans watched closely, copying Osbourne's movements when he performed the equally large Falstaff in Verdi's opera.

The Albion Colliery in 1965, showing the stables on the right which were used as a mortuary following the 1894 disaster.

Albion Colliery and Cilfynydd, pictured on a snowy day, *c.* 1966. In 1928, the Albion Steam Coal Co. went into liquidation and the assets were purchased by the Powell Dyffryn Steam Coal Co. It remained in their ownership until nationalization in 1947 when 996 men were employed. Production ceased in 1966.

The site of the former Albion Colliery in 1976. The building on the left was all that remained of the engine house of the downcast shaft.

Albert Owen, a winder at the Albion Colliery, during the recovery of the reusable equipment which followed the closure of the pit in 1966. He is pictured standing next to the winder, on which the lives of the colliers depended twice daily yet which they rarely saw, belonging as it did to the world of the colliery engineer. This winding engine could lower or raise a cage of miners at 30ft per second but ran at 60ft per second when raising coal.

The site of the former Albion Colliery in the 1970s. The photograph shows the capping of the two shafts in 1972. The colliery is now the site of Coedylan Comprehensive School.

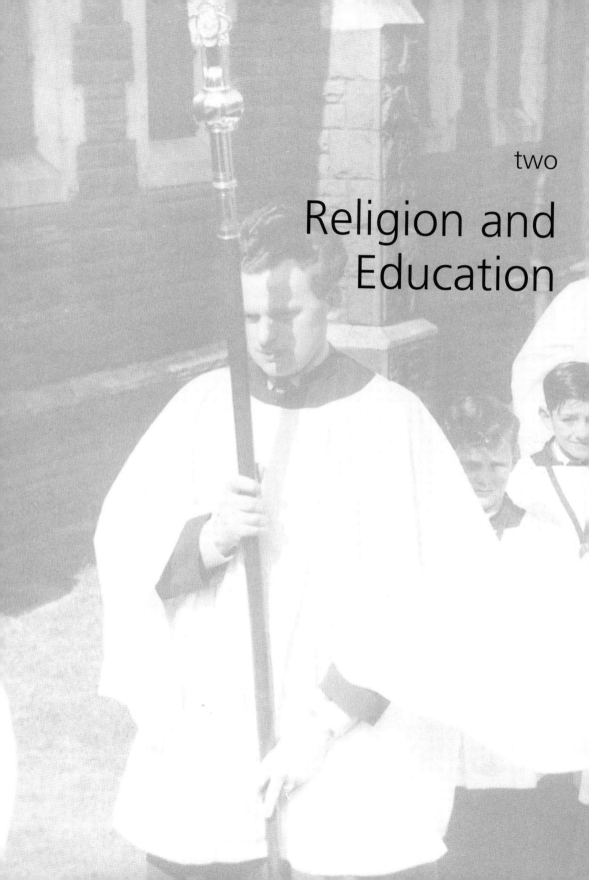

two

Religion and Education

St Luke's church on Howell Street. The church was dedicated by Richard Lewis, Bishop of Llandaff, on 28 February 1893. It was part of the parish of Eglwysilan until 1913, when Cilfynydd became a conventional district, with Revd R.T. Howells as priest in charge. He was followed by the Revd J.R. James who in turn was succeeded by the Revd Illtyd Jones in 1920.

St Luke's Mothers' Union, with the Cilfynydd Billiard Hall in the background and Dr Tudor Williams' Dundella House on the right.

St Luke's church choir, with Revd J. Morgan, in 1955.

A Christmas party held at St Luke's church, *c.* 1958. The vicar, Revd J. Morgan, is pictured on the left.

Beulah English Baptist church, Wood Street, after the extension to the front of the building in 1937. The importance of religion in the village can be seen by the erection of chapels as a priority. In Cilfynydd they even preceded the school. The church and chapels were always filled to capacity and the religious revival of 1905, led by Evan Roberts, spurred the congregation to even greater zeal. Indeed Roberts even preached once in Bethel Chapel.

Beulah Sunday school outing, *c.* 1915. The chapels were cultural centres with their annual operettas, cantatas, oratorios and other musical events. By 1920, Cilfynydd even had a converted shop in Richard Street where the Plymouth Brethren met. The decline in chapel-going began after the Second World War, and at the time of writing this book only St Luke's and Beulah Chapels still exist.

Beulah outing on a horse-drawn brake, having a rest in Cowbridge on the way to Porthcawl. The trip included Mr and Mrs Andrew Holland, Mr and Mrs W.J. Williams, Mrs Jenny Leonard, Mrs Elizabeth Gulliford, Miss Florrie Leonard, Mr Brenig Roberts (a well-known organist) and tenor Mr James Hunt.

The congregation of Beulah English Baptist church celebrate the completion of the new extension in 1937.

Beulah English Baptist church outing to Porthcawl in 1930.

Bethel Calvinistic Methodist Chapel, William Street. Built in 1887, the first minister was Revd Michael Williams who remained there for thirty-five years. The chapel averaged 400 members and one of its ministers, Revd David Owen Jones, won the crown at the Royal National Eisteddfod, Fishguard, in 1936 for one of his poems. The chapel deacons, particularly Jones Taylor, had a great influence over the children and their spiritual education. Before chapels were built in Cilfynydd worshippers had to travel to Pontypridd. The Calvinistic Methodists attended Penuel, and members recognised the need for facilities in Cilfynydd. Prayer meetings and a Sunday school were held at No. 46 William Street, Cilfynydd, under the guidance of Penuel members.

The manse of Bethel Calvinistic Methodist Chapel on William Street. The Revd William Lewis of Penuel was the prime mover of the Bethel cause, and in 1887 a vestry was opened. This soon developed into a thriving Sunday school of nearly 100 scholars with eleven teachers. Shortly afterwards, the chapel was built at a cost of £1,400. It was officially opened in May 1889 with a membership of 160. The chapel closed in the 1980s and was demolished in 1988.

Moriah Welsh Congregational Chapel, Ann Street. Moriah started out as a branch of Seion, Pontypridd, which in 1887 assisted members who lived in Cilfynydd to build a vestry where they might hold their own services. The vestry served as Cilfynydd's original primary school and ninety-four pupils were admitted on 15 August 1887. The Moriah vestry continued to be used until the school was built in 1889. Attendance at the vestry grew, too, and Moriah was founded as a church in 1888. The foundations of the chapel were laid in 1889 and it opened in 1891 under the minister Revd R.B. Williams.

Moriah Young People on a trip to Ystradfellte, *c*. 1938. From left to right: Aeron Lewis (later Registrar at the University of Wales, Cardiff), Brynmor Jones (later divisional education officer), Elwyn Owen (chemist shop owner, Richard Street), -?-, Whitfield Jones, Olwen Jones, Marjorie Owen, Edryd Lewis, John Pugh, Brenda Davies (later married to Sir Geraint Evans), Gareth Owen (became principal of University College Aberystwyth), Bray Lewis, Revd John Francis, -?-, Morfydd Lewis, Janet Evans, Meirion Owen, Brinley Edwards.

Left: Rehoboth Welsh Baptist Chapel on Cilfynydd Road was built as a branch of Tabernacl chapel, Pontypridd. The vestry was built and opened in 1888 and the main body of the chapel opened in May 1889 with a membership of 129. The chapel closed in 1979 and was subsequently demolished.

Opposite above: An outing for the members of Rehoboth Chapel, *c*. 1940. Annual seaside trips were popular with the chapel-goers; Porthcawl and Barry Island were favourite destinations. Such trips have been beautifully described by many of Wales's popular poets, but none have quite captured the events as well as the writer Gwyn Thomas.

Primitive Methodist church, Howell Street. Cilfynydd's chapels were built around the same time and in quite similar circumstances. Some chapels held their earliest prayer meetings in the homes of their members. Howell Street Primitive Methodist church founders, including the Seymours, Tomans and Cullens, quickly discovered that their homes were not large enough to accommodate all who wished to attend. Prayer meetings were held in the loft of a bake house at the bottom of Richard Street before the chapel was built in 1890.

The interior of Bethany Calvinistic Methodist Chapel on Cilfynydd Road, *c.* 1900. The chapel was next door to Richard's Hotel; a house now occupies the site.

Richard Williams of Tonyrefail, headmaster of Cilfynydd Boys' School between 1887 and 1928. With the influx of so many families and the need for primary education for their children, a school was opened in the vestry of Moriah Welsh Congregational Chapel. On 15 August 1887 ninety-four pupils were admitted and a further thirteen were enlisted before the weekend. Richard Williams, aged twenty-four, a graduate of the University College of South Wales and Monmouthshire in Cardiff, was the only teacher and headteacher. Moriah had a small room – 40ft long by 20ft wide – which was totally inadequate for teaching 100 children, so many of the younger ones were moved to Bethel. Eglwysilan School Board met on 28 November 1887 and appointed Janet Davies as an assistant. They also agreed to purchase an acre of land, costing £475. A school was built to accommodate 630 children at a cost of £5,320. On 2 April 1889, Alfred Thomas MP officially opened the three single-story buildings for boys, infants and girls. In 1899 an upper floor was added to the boys' and girls' departments.

Cilfynydd School, *c.* 1960. The building to the left was the original boys' school, with the infants' school in the centre and the girls' school to the right.

A class of girls from Cilfynydd School, 1905. The first entry in the new school logbook read: 'I Richard Williams opened the above temporary school on the 15th day of August 1887. I admitted 94 children and out of the number 45 in a very backward state, not even knowing their letters. The greater number of these had not been in any school before. The others who attended school had not been able to attend half their time, owing to the great distance they had to walk. The parents of a great part of the children are that of migrating class who never stay long in the same place, consequently their children are generally found to be extremely backward.'

A class of boys from Cilfynydd School, 1905. At this time the official age range for attending was 5–14 years old, although it could sometimes be younger. With a growing population in the village, the school numbers increased and by 1909 had reached a peak of 996 on the register.

Staff from Cilfynydd School, c. 1910. A few boys and girls from here went to the Pontypridd Grammar School but the remainder could sit a school-leaving certificate at the age of fourteen. Most boys then went to work in the Albion Colliery.

St David's Day, 1915. A detached house was built next to the school called the Cookery Centre, where girls were taught the rudiments of housework – such as cleaning, laundry and cookery – one day per week. The boys were sent to a woodwork centre in the grounds of Pontsionnorton School. This system continued until the end of the Second World War except that many more children went on to study at the Pontypridd Boys' or Girls' Grammar School or to Mill Street Central School.

St David's Day, 1915. The headteachers of Cilfynydd School since its opening were: Richard Williams (1887-1928), John Phillips (1928-35), Mr Gabriel (1935-43), D.J. Griffiths (1943-?), Tom Burrows (?-1960), Meurig Evans (1961-1966), Tom Morgan (1966-71), William Hargest (1971-82), Alun Caffrey (1982-2004) and Gareth Bowen (2004-present).

Cilfynydd Boys' School Rugby Team, 1929/30. The headmaster in the centre of the picture is John Phillips, a stout disciplinarian who, due to his Italian looks, was known as Bracchi. The teachers, standing left to right, are: Evan Felix, Susie Davies, David John Griffiths, Mr Evans, -?-, David Davies, -?-, and Tom Burrows. The 1944 Education Act saw the school leaving age raised to fifteen and children over eleven years of age who had not passed any examinations became pupils of Cilfynydd Secondary School, where Mr Chambers was headmaster. The boys' and girls' schools, aged seven to eleven years, combined to form Cilfynydd Junior School.

Staff from Cilfynydd Infants' School, c. 1959. From left to right, back row: Mrs Ellis, Eva Paget, Blodwen Evans. Front row: Miss Hughes, -?-, Mrs Steel. In the mid-1950s the secondary school closed and the pupils were transferred to Coedylan Seconday School.

Children from Mr Tawelfryn Edwards' class at Cilfynydd Primary School in 1959. Mr Edwards is pictured on the left while the headmaster, Tom Burrows, is on the right. Mr Burrows was one of six children born at No. 71 William Street. His sisters were Jenny, Kitty and Gladys and he had two brothers named Charlie and Albert, whose son is operatic tenor Stuart Burrows.

A presentation to Miss Beatrice Abraham, dinner lady, on her retirement, made by the headmistress of the infants' school, Miss Blodwen Evans, in 1961. The male staff, standing from left to right, are: David Davies, Tom Morgan, Tawelfryn Edwards, William Hargest, Meurig Evans (headmaster). Female staff: Mrs Muriel Gair, Mrs Jenkins, Miss Abraham, Mrs Cummings (dinner lady), Mrs Steele, Miss B. Evans, Miss Hughes, Miss Davies, Mrs Jones, -?-, Mrs Eva Paget.

Standard IV at Cilfynydd Primary School, 1962, pictured with teacher Miss Marged Jenkins and headteacher Meurig Evans.

St David's Day, 1966. In 1962 the junior and infant departments combined to become the present Cilfynydd County Primary School.

three

Tragedy and Triumph

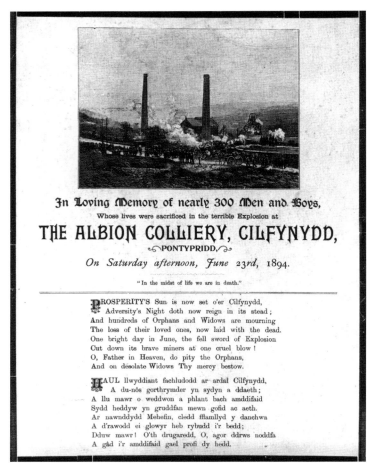

In Loving Memory of nearly 300 Men and Boys,

Whose lives were sacrificed in the terrible Explosion at

THE ALBION COLLIERY, CILFYNYDD,

PONTYPRIDD,

On Saturday afternoon, June 23rd, 1894.

"In the midst of life we are in death."

PROSPERITY'S Sun is now set o'er Cilfynydd,
Adversity's Night doth now reign in its stead ;
And hundreds of Orphans and Widows are mourning
The loss of their loved ones, now laid with the dead.
One bright day in June, the fell sword of Explosion
Cut down its brave miners at one cruel blow !
O, Father in Heaven, do pity the Orphans,
And on desolate Widows Thy mercy bestow.

HAUL llwyddiant fachludodd ar ardal Cilfynydd,
A du-nôs gorthrymder yn sydyn a ddaeth ;
A llu mawr o weddwon a phlant bach amddifaid
Sydd heddyw yn gruddfan mewn gofid ac aeth.
Ar nawnddydd Mehefin, cledd fflamllyd y danchwa
A d'rawodd ei glowyr heb rybudd i'r bedd;
Dduw mawr ! O'th drugaredd, O, agor ddrws noddfa
A gâd i'r amddifaid gael profi dy hedd.

Albion Colliery disaster, 23 June 1894. By the end of the day the village had 150 widows and 350 fatherless children. At 2 p.m., the Saturday shift descended into the pit to carry out cleaning and repair work. As shoppers crowded Richard Street at 3.50 p.m., two loud explosions were heard above ground in quick succession. It was followed by a charge of dust and smoke from the downcast and then the upcast shaft. Men on the surface were blown backwards and although they felt the heat they saw no flames. Colliery manager Philip Jones and his son, acting under-manager William Jones, joined James Groves the pitman and William Garnett the night fireman to descend the shaft. The village doctor, Dr Lyttle, was soon on the scene and during the next twenty-four hours just sixteen men were brought out alive, but only five survived.

Opposite below: Women and children rushed to the Albion Colliery to see if their loved ones had survived. The hayloft above the stables in the colliery became a temporary morgue, guarded by two policemen. By 9.15 p.m. on Saturday the first of the dead were brought up. Many of the victims were badly mutilated and were laid in rows covered by blankets. By 10 p.m. there were harrowing scenes as relatives desperately searched for family members by lantern light. Miraculously, George Bumford, David Lewis and George Martin were brought out alive. By noon on Sunday, 103 bodies had been recovered. A police force of sixty men drafted from Merthyr, Llandaff and Canton arrived to control the crowds who tried to cross the humpbacked bridge to gain access to the colliery.

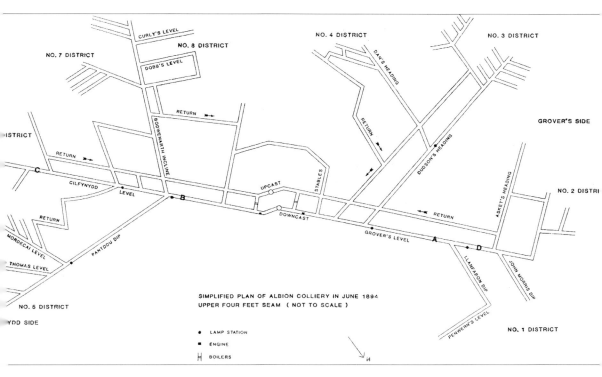

Above: A simplified plan of the Albion Colliery, 1894. Nobody was sure how many men were underground at the time of the disaster, but the final tally was 295. At 11 p.m. J.T. Robson arrived from Swansea and two assistant inspectors, F.A. Gray and J. Dyer Lewis, descended the shaft to join William Lewis, the agent, and J. Mansel Sims, another assistant inspector. By 3 a.m. the party penetrated as far as the double parting on the Grover's side and then down the Llanfabon dip only to be confronted with some horrific sights. By Sunday evening Joseph S. Martin began his examination of the origin of the explosion.

A drayman is seen bringing beer to the village to supply 2,000 spectators. Special trains were even put on. One indirect effect of the disaster was the consumption of beer which was so great that ten days after the disaster a meeting of the East Glamorgan Welsh Baptist Association held at Merthyr Tydfil said, 'we condemn in most unequivocal terms the conduct of certain persons in sending dray loads of beer to Cilfynydd...' Inns opened illegally on the Sunday while the chapels closed. Miners' leader William Abraham (Mabon) arrived and the home secretary Asquith wrote to Robson, Her Majesty's inspector of mines, saying: 'The Queen is much shocked at the news of the sad disaster at Cilfynydd and of the terrible loss of life. Her majesty commands me to convey her deep sympathy to the families and relatives of those who have been lost. She has heard of the brave efforts to save life and awaits with anxiety the results of further explorations.' The secretary of the South Wales and Monmouthshire Miners Permanent Provident Society, estimated the disaster would cost £70,000 and £5 was given to relatives to help pay for the funeral expenses. He went to Richard Street post office and sent telegrams to three undertakers in Pontypridd and one in Cardiff asking for 250 coffins of the 'finest elm' with the expense to be borne by the Albion Steam Coal Co. *Western Mail* reporter, Morien, said it was like arriving in a city 'struck by a plague' since windows were all curtained and carts travelled through carrying coffins. One of those who died was a ticket-of-leave convict who had to report regularly to the police at Pontypridd. In death his criminal record was not revealed and although he was named with other victims, his real identity has been respected to this day.

IN AFFECTIONATE REMEMBRANCE

OF

EVAN,

BELOVED SON OF ISAAC AND MARGARET DAVIS,

Who was killed by an Explosion at the Albion Colliery, Cilfynydd,

South Wales, June 23rd, 1894,

AGED 15 YEARS.

———

INTERRED AT GLYNTAFF CEMETERY, JUNE 28th, 1894.

Memorial card to an Albion Colliery disaster victim. On the following Monday an inquest opened at the New Inn, Pontypridd. Pontypridd Burial Board met to make arrangements, and in the House of Commons expressions of sympathy were offered by various speakers including Keir Hardie. Various bodies promised donations, including £1,000 from the Albion Steam Coal Co. On the Tuesday the chairman of the Albion Steam Coal Co., Mathew Cope, accompanied by Henry Lewis, arrived from Antwerp where they were on holiday with their families.

Revd Hugh Phillip Morgan (1866-1946). He came to Cilfynydd in 1890 from Pontrhydygroes and became a lay preacher, serving an apprenticeship with the Revd John Evans of Eglwysbach Chapel in Pontypridd. He was at the same time the sub-editor of *Y Tarian*, a Welsh magazine. He was highly praised for staying in the loft of the stables of the Albion Colliery for many days helping the bereaved families to claim the bodies of the victims. It must have been a harrowing time, for more than once, because of the terrible injuries, a body was returned to the loft in the hope it might be correctly identified. Shortly after the disaster he emigrated to the USA. His sister, Caroline Lewis, kept shops in Wood Street and Richard Street and finally at No. 88 Mary Street. She died at the age of ninety-three, having raised twelve children.

Funeral procession towards Glyntaff cemetery. Preparations took place in Llanfabon churchyard to bury some of the dead, and forty men were sent by the Albion Co. to dig graves in a section of the cemetery. Glyntaff cemetery held funerals for the first group of workmen, which included a group of Catholic workers from Treforest. The service was conducted by Fathers Noonan and McManus. On a hot Wednesday, the first of the mass funerals took place with a procession moving along Jones Street, past the colliery and on to Llanfabon. Men accompanied the coffins walking four abreast with bearers changing every few hundred yards.

Funeral procession, 1894. There were forty-one bodies in this cortege. The sun reflected on brass nameplates and all that could be heard was the shuffling of feet and sobbing. Many bodies went by train to North Wales, Cardiganshire and the Rhondda. Richard Jones of Penparc, Cardigan, was buried just two weeks after starting work. By Wednesday, 242 bodies had been identified with twenty more remaining unidentified in the loft. At 6 p.m. an exploration party of fifty-two miners went into the pit to try and work out how to dispose of the 118 horses that had died. They were buried in the slag heap behind Mary Street. Superintendent Jones ordered eleven unidentified bodies be buried in Llanfabon. Fifteen other victims were buried in the churchyard, attended by a crowd of 500, and fifty-three were buried in Glyntaff. Moriah Chapel lost forty members in the disaster. A week after the disaster a further seven victims were found and on Sunday notices were displayed asking people if they had relatives missing. Houses became vacant as widows moved out to relatives and the school closed for a month because attendance was so low. As late as 6 August another two unidentified bodies were found.

This photograph was taken shortly after the Albion disaster of 1894. Crowds can be seen on the main road and around the downcast shaft. The inquest into the Albion Disaster ran from 16-20 and 24-27 July 1894. The coroners were E.B. Reece of Cardiff and R.J. Rhys of Aberdare, sitting with a jury of seventeen 'intelligent gentlemen'. The government was represented by barrister J. Roskill, appointed by the secretary of state at the Home Office. The jury's verdict was that they lost their lives due to an explosion of gas, accelerated by coal dust. The origins of the explosion were unsure, but short-firing was practiced without sufficient precautions to safety.

A group of Cilfynydd miners, c. 1897. Third from the left in the front row is George Bumford who survived the Albion disaster. During the inquest it was obvious the Coal Mines Regulation Act of 1887 had been contravened. As far as negligence was concerned, two offences were to be dealt with: blasting timbers during shifts and not watering the mine to lay dust. Because they failed to ascertain where the explosion occurred, Roskill concluded he could not recommend a prosecution for manslaughter. When it came to watering the mine he said evidence was not strong enough to justify criminal proceedings against anyone. Manager Phillip Jones was indicted for storing or allowing storage of explosives and fined £10. William Anstes was also indicted on the same charge and fined £2. The pit was in full production again by October 1894 producing 45,000 tons of coal a month.

William Abraham (Mabon), president of the South Wales Miner's Federation, unveiling a monument in Llanfabon cemetery on 1 July 1907 in memory of the eleven unknown victims of the Albion Colliery disaster.

Richard Street following the tornado of Monday 27 October 1913. Less than two weeks after the Senghenydd Colliery disaster, a terrifying storm swept the Pontypridd area, causing widespread destruction and two deaths. The wind rose at 4.30 p.m., with a 'troubled sky', before rain began to fall at 5.20 p.m., followed by the first flash of red lightning five minutes later. There followed intense blue lightning, flashing at frequent intervals, accompanied by a little thunder. By 5.50 p.m. a hissing sound was heard, with heat and air pressure becoming oppressive.

Richard Street following the tornado. The storm passed through Llantwit Fardre, Treforest and Glyntaff, blowing down trees and chimney stacks, smashing windows and tearing roofs apart. By the time it reached Cilfynydd it was 200 yards wide and swept through the village from south to north, causing further devastation to Edwardsville and Abercynon. When it reached Howell Street it tore off the corrugated roof, attached to steel arches, of the local branch of the Ynysybwl Co-operative Society. Some of the roof was found a mile away on Graig Evan Leyshon Common.

The village shops in Richard Street were badly damaged, with goods strewn over the road and most of the roofs destroyed altogether. Evan Prosser, a haulier, was blown thirty yards into the Glamorganshire Canal and survived. Sadly, Thomas John Harries of Oakland Terrace was found dead in a field after being hurled 400 yards.

A scene near the police station on Cilfynydd Road following the storm. The tornado continued on its destructive path towards Abercynon and Edwardsville, where it reached its peak by blowing down most of the tombstones in the churchyard. The buildings on the right, which were opposite the police station, belonged to the Glamorganshire Canal. In the distance can be seen part of the steel structure of the bridge leading to Cilfynydd railway station.

Rehoboth Chapel following the tornado. The entire north side of the chapel was blown inwards by the force of the storm. Every chapel roof in the village was also damaged by the tornado. Chimney stacks were destroyed in almost every home. The final cost of repairs throughout the Taff Vale area amounted to £40,000, which was a substantial sum in 1913.

The rear of Cilfynydd Road following the storm. The first house (No. 5) was at this time occupied by Mr Curtis, a photographer who took many local views, including these of the tornado. Later on the house became a small shop and café known as the Coffee Tavern. In the top right-hand corner is a warehouse belonging to the Glamorganshire Canal Co. and a hand-operated crane alongside lock No. 25, also known as Ynyscaedudwg Lock. These houses were prone to flooding from Nantcaedudwg which flowed under the road and canal before turning south west to join the river Taff. Today the stream is piped to the river along this section.

Jones Street following the tornado. One resident claimed: 'First there was a hissing noise, then a rustling noise growing louder and louder into a roar.' For further details on the storm, see 'A South Wales Tornado' by Meurig Evans in *Glamorgan Historian*, Vol. XI.

Above: The roofs of the houses in Park Place were completely destroyed. Opposite the entrance to the Albion Colliery stood the office of the local branch of the Miners' Federation, a wooden building on heavy tram wheels. The whole structure was swept away. A house, owned by the chairman of the Federation, Abraham Lewis, had its roof demolished and furniture damaged. His next-door neighbour, John Jones, managed to save a baby seconds before collapsing debris destroyed the bedroom.

Left: The incredible power of the tornado forced a man's jacket through the wooden panels of a door in Wood Street.

Above: Numbers 42 and 43 Wood Street following the storm. When the tornado hit, considerable damage occurred to all the houses, and sheds and henhouses in allotment gardens disappeared without trace.

Right: Captain D.T. Tanner of the 16th Battalion of the Royal Welch Fusiliers. A teacher at Cilfynydd School, he patriotically responded to his country's call in October 1914. He met his death in France on 31 August 1916.

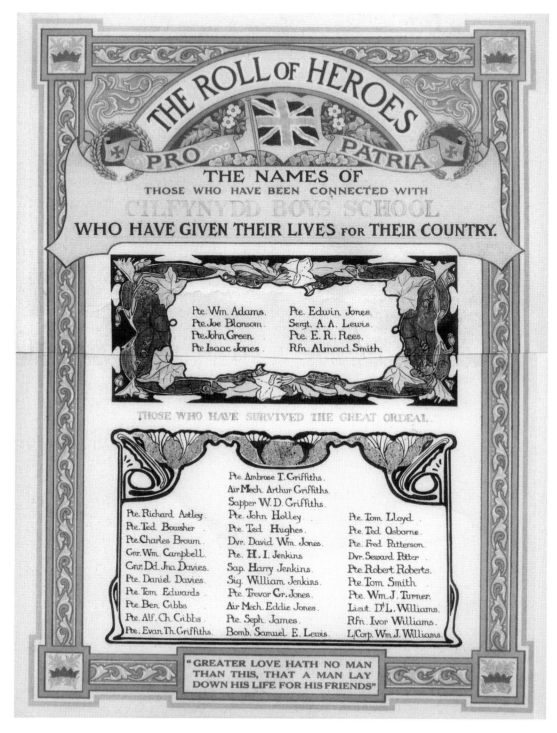

The Roll of Heroes, 1918. This gives the names of those associated with Cilfynydd Boys' School who gave their lives for their country during the First World War.

Above left: The Powell brothers, Donald (1928-2004), William (1931-39) and Alan (1936-2004), were three of Tom and May Powell's five children, who lived at Oakland Crescent. Donald eventually settled in Rhydyfelin with his wife Barbara and three children and became a successful author of two books on the history of Pontypridd. Alan, the first baby born at the newly built Oakland Crescent in 1936, raised two children with his wife Gwyneth in nearby Oakland Terrace. On 11 October 1939, the Powell family suffered a terrible tragedy when William (Billy) was killed by a lorry close to King's Garage on Cilfynydd Road, aged eight. A platoon of the Royal Artillery, in which his father Tom was serving, marched alongside the funeral cortege to Glyntaff cemetery.

Above right: Thomas Powell (1909-73) from Oakland Crescent. Thomas (Tom) was born in Pantygraigwen, one of eleven children to William Powell, originally from Brecon, and Mary Rogers from Scranton, Pensylvannia, USA. In 1928, he married May Fishbourne of Gwaelod y Garth and the couple set up home in Ivor Court, a group of houses close to where the present gates of Ynysangharad War Memorial Park in Pontypridd now stand. He was a collier in Pontypridd during his youth and was trapped when part of the pit roof collapsed before being rescued. He was later called up to the Royal Artillery at the start of the Second World War. Private Powell (no. 3906348) was a member of the 239 battery of the 77th Anti-Aircraft Gunners. He was captured by the Japanese in Sumatra in 1942 and spent the next three years surviving the most horrendous conditions as a prisoner of war in Java. By 1945 he weighed little more than six stone and was deaf in one ear as a result of being beaten with the butt of a rifle from a Japanese guard for trying to steal a potato because he was starving. Once the camp was liberated he returned home to his wife and four children, suffering from malaria and malnutrition, and spent several months in hospital in Chepstow. He eventually returned to Cilfynydd and worked for a while at various factories on Treforest Industrial Estate before developing cancer and losing his brave battle at the age of just sixty-four.

Cilfynydd 'C' Company 2nd Battalion Glamorgan Home Guard under Capt. Jack Howells, pictured on the bowling green, Cilfynydd, in 1942. Many members of the Home Guard worked in the mines and field exercise became enjoyable events during weekends. The waste slip from Abercynon Colliery was the range where Molotov cocktails or phosphorous bombs were fired. A very wet weekend in 1943 saw the company under canvas in Penycoedcae where on the Sunday morning hand grenade throwing was to be exercised. Most spent Saturday evening in the Queen's Hotel before returning, wet inside and out, to their tents for the night. From left to right, front row: Cpl Herbie Vale, Cpl Charles Gibbs, Sgt Dai Butler, Sgt Garnet Corbet, Sgt Tommy Williams, Lt Johnny Roberts, Capt. Jack Howells, Capt. Vincent Price, Maj. W.E.R. Edwards, Dr Thomas (Abercynon), Lt Charles Burgess, Sgt-Maj. Will Howells, Sgt-Maj. Bert Meets, Sgt Joe Jones, Sgt Edward Williams, Sgt Ivor Lloyd, Sgt Hugh Hamer. Second row: Alec Smith, Greg Bannon, Ron Reel, Edgar Thomas, Jimmy Rochford, Ernie Gordon, Victor Thomas, Ted Ebsworth, Jackie Campbell, Dai John Rees, Billy Morgan, Tommy Price, Ernie Walby, Ray Thomas, Tom Griffiths, Owen Hughes. Third row: Elwyn Woods, Glyn Jones, Tudor Burton, Joe Male, Henry Elliot, Tom Griffiths, Reg Williams, Cliff Rowley, Jim Rees, Harry Rowbotham, Danny Harries, Idris Howells, Mel Adams, Harold Tarr, Bob Roberts, Fred Rowley, Idwal Owen. Fourth row: Tommy Gooch, Ted Mathews, Dai Barratt, Richard Gibbs, David Davies, Brynmor Owen, Cyril Kemp, Will Barratt, Joe Evans, David (Joe) Male, Lionel Davies, John Strawsfield, Arthur Evans, Bryn Walters, Joe Morgan, Edward Pearce, Brian Holly, Denzil Thomas, Baden Gough, Glyn Gough, Cadfan Owen. Fifth row: Arnold Butler, Islwyn Snooks, Elwyn Owen, Trevor Butler, Tom Welland, Cyril Bill, Dai Jones, Gwyn Wheelan, Bob Bevan, Sam Rees, Charlie Doel, Alwyn Pritchard, Graham Davies, Douglas Doel, George Weaver, Lawrence Gibbs, Glyn Pritchard, Ronnie Male, Aneurin Pitt. Sixth row: Frank Rowbotham, William Rowe, Albert Howells, Wyndham Gough, Kenny Edwards, Harry Bowsher, Richard Ashley, Syd Boyles, Ernie Williams, Harvey Edwards, Tommy Jenkins, Ivor Rowe, David Davies, William Davies, Jackie Manning, Tudor Rosser, Billy Mills. Back row: Ben Davies, Elias Jones, Evan Wilcox, Richie Burns, Edgar Barrett, Emrys Peck, Evan Jones, Will Jones, Alfred Matthews, Mieron Owen, Ivor Jones Penwen, Dai Matthews, Tommy James, Ivor Jones, Russell Bennett, Owen Hughes, Reg Goddard, Danny Allen.

Opposite below: Bank slippage at Cilfynydd. This photograph, dating from around 1920, shows the partly drained canal relieving the pressure on the towpath where the bank has collapsed again. The railway to the colliery can be seen with the river Taff alongside. On the towpath, in the distance, was a hand-operated winch; a chain ran from the winch to a manhole cover in the bed of the canal. This acted like a large plug to empty the canal when needed. The houses near King's Garage on Cilfynydd Road can be seen. The abandoned canal boat was still there when the A470 dual carriageway was built fifty years later. This line of the canal is immediately under the south-bound lane of the carriageway.

Above: Part of the bank alongside the Taff Vale railway, slipped in 1915. This section of the Glamorganshire Canal, where it clung to the hillsides, was prone to collapse. The result of the slip meant canal boats could go no further.

Above: Bodwenarth Terrace during the flood of 1910. Notice the extent of the flood, which has totally washed away the road revealing the drainage system below.

Right: Damage caused by flooding, from Howell Street to the side of the Albion Hotel. Frequent water damage eventually led to the demise of the public house on Cilfynydd Road.

Below: Flood damage at the top of Oakland Terrace. With so much water running off the mountain side, it comes as little wonder why residents later worried about their own safety since the huge spoil tip was high above them.

Opposite below: A group of housewives desperately try to salvage what they can from a house on Cilfynydd Road following floods in 1955. This was one of the houses threatened by Nantcaedudwg.

The Billiard Hall on fire, 1981. This is where most of the village's young men learnt to play snooker and billiards, including such excellent players as Bert Toomey. It was also a place to discuss the political issues of the day. Discipline in the hall, built from wood, was very strict. Two of the supervisors were Dick Jones, the caretaker of the Workmen's Hall, and Dick Rees (Penwern) who hobbled around on two sticks. Cilfynydd's so-called 'political expert' at the Billiard Hall was Brenig Roberts, who gave his views on everything. Two other characters were the Jenkins brothers, Ben and Llew. Both were committed communists. Ben was a fervid revolutionary who could rouse any gathering while Llew was the quiet philosopher.

A group of school friends from around the village, *c.* 1934. In the back row is Dorcas Bennett, with Marie Evans (Bryn Road) and Geraint Evans (William Street) in the middle. The two children in the front row are Thelma Griffiths of Mary Street and Audrey Davies of Oakland Terrace.

Neighbours from Mary Street gathered to celebrate the Coronation of King George VI in 1937.

Bedw Terrace celebrations, 1945. The end of the Second World War was received with great relief and enjoyment. Although there was a shortage of food and other commodities every street managed to hold a party.

Celebrating the end of the Second World War in Bedw Terrace, 1945.

A Victory Party was held in the Unemployed Hall on Park Place to celebrate the end of the Second World War in 1945

Wood Street celebrations, 1948. Whether it be a Coronation, or the end of war, Wood Street residents were the first to raise funds and commemorate a special event. Wood Street also often celebrated the sporting success of their boxing neighbour, Cecil Brown.

Cilfynydd Workmen's Hall presentation, March 1950. Councillor Emrys Peck is shaking hands with Thomas Evans before presenting him with a clock to mark his thirty years service as treasurer of Cilfynydd Workmen's Institute. From left to right: Mr Jones, Vince Griffiths, Gomer Harris, Emrys Peck, Mr Watkins, Verdun Housler, -?-, Thomas Evans, Mr Rees, George Thomas, Mr Jones and Dillwyn Coleman.

Festival of Britain celebrations in Bedw Terrace, 1951.

Coronation celebrations, 1953. Cilfynydd held a carnival and sports day in June 1953 to mark the Coronation of Queen Elizabeth II. A service of song was held in Moriah Welsh Congregational Chapel on 31 May with Edryd Lewis as conductor assisted by the Beulah Sisterhood Choir. On Tuesday 2 June 'A Best Decorated Street' competition was held by Pontypridd Urban District Council. The advertising poster read: 'The Council requests every home to show its loyalty to the Crown by decorating their windows with flags and bunting, and also decorate their streets for which they have three prizes of £5, £3 and £2 for the best decorated street.'

Bedw Terrace coronation party, 2 June 1953. At 3 p.m. the local carnival queen and her court ladies toured Norton Bridge via Bedw Terrace, and through the streets to Heol y Mynydd. The queen was Heather Hughes from Wood Street, with her ladies Valerie Rees from Ann Street, Olwen Jones from Pontsionnorton, Arfona Williams from Cilfynydd Road and Brenda Hope from Richard Street

A party held at Bethany Chapel vestry in 1955. From left to right, standing: Mrs M. Rees, William Wilde, Mr M. Burton, Mr W. Gray, Mrs N. Bowsher, Mrs M. Knight, Elvira Rees and the children of the congregation.

Visitors to the Albion Colliery, *c.* 1950. It became a regular feature for workers to take small groups of visitors down the shaft on a Sunday. This picture shows well-known Richard Street café owner Tony Carini, with friends including Mostyn Jones, Ken Thomas, Ron Male and Owen Thomas. For young boys it often proved a memorable experience, for they were told that if they didn't work hard at school then this could be the conditions in which they would work for the rest of their lives.

Beulah English Baptist church Christmas party in 1960.

four

Sport and Leisure

The cast of Beulah Chapel's performance of the cantata *The Magic Ruby, c.* 1925. Choirs were associated with each chapel and frequently competed in Eisteddfodau. Essays, poetry and recitation competitions were also a feature of the Eisteddfod. Every chapel performed oratorios and children's operas annually.

Cilfynydd Juvenile Boys' Choir, 1926. The choir, formed under the baton of William Wilde, helped raise funds for the miners during the 1926 General Strike. They travelled to London for a prestigious concert at the Royal Albert Hall. From left to right, back row: Gwlithyn Evans (later organist in Moriah Chapel and then organist at St Woollos church, Newport), Trevor Jones (Dick Mantle), Dai John Rees, Tecwyn James, Billy John Griffiths, Con Waffington, Trevor Jones, Emlyn Butler, Nono Hughes. Third row: Alec Smith, Thomas Jones, Billy Lloyd, Tommy Smith, Emrys Lloyd, Neville Howells. Second row: Merddyn James, Dewi Morgan, Dai Davies, Billy Wilde, Richard Owen, Jackie MacAlister. Front row: Elvet Howells, Donald MacAlister, Freddie Hughes, Islwyn Wilde, Bob Roberts, Howard Bennett.

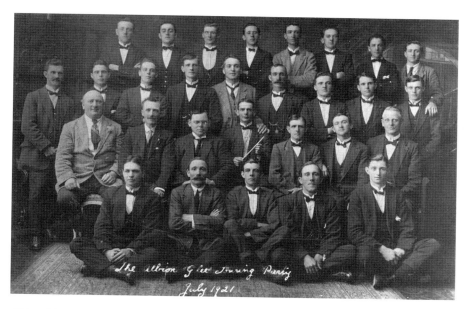

Albion Glee Touring Party, July 1921. Pictured is conductor William Daniel Wilde, one-time choirmaster at Bethany Chapel. Mr Wilde was the illegitimate son of a Rhondda headmaster and was brought up by his grandparents. He married Sarah and the couple had thirteen children. Sally, the eldest, married local councillor Emrys Peck. In the basement of his house he ran a small printing business and also composed a phenomenal amount of operettas and songs. He also showed silent films in a small shed next to his house, with the following notice on his letterheaded notepaper reading: 'Entertainments given in 9.5mm and 16mm'. Also pictured in the front row on the right is William John Evans, born in 1903, later to become a well-known conductor in his own right who led the Handel Glee Party, Cilfynydd Male Voice Choir and the famous Cor Meibion Pontypridd. Known as Stripes (because he wore striped trousers), his son was Sir Geraint Evans. The Handel Glee Party was a successful entity, with such choristers as Emlyn Kemp, Llew Harris, 'Ianto Gas', Teifi Evans and 'Snowy Jones.'

Madam Sara Elin Harrison, *c.* 1915. This fine musician was the daughter of John Phillips, a boot maker from Richard Street, who wrote the Welsh version of *Silent Night*. It was the first item performed publicly by Stuart Burrows at the age of ten in Bethel chapel. Madam Harrison was the conductor of the Cilfynydd Philharmonic Society, a successful mixed choral society made up of the congregations of several chapels in the village. A local piano teacher, one of her pupils was a young Geraint Evans, and it was she who invited him to give his first performance of *Elijah* while only seventeen years of age at the Workmen's Hall. When Sir Geraint was the subject of *This Is Your Life*, Madam Harrison made a surprise entrance on the popular television programme. She later married tenor Jack Howells.

A poster for the Cilfynydd & District Amateur Dramatic Society's production of the *Deep Blue Sea* by Terrence Rattigan, at the Workmen's Hall in 1957. For many years the society produced stage plays of the highest calibre, winning massive acclaim in the local press. Such was the success of the *Deep Blue Sea* that it went on 'tour' to Nelson and Bedlinog. The cast was overjoyed when one of the members, Don Powell, received a letter from actor Kenneth More. It said: 'As an "old Boy" of the original production I am greatly interested in any revival of what I consider to be Rattigan's finest play. If you add to this interest at least four quarts of pure Welsh blood, Cardiff variety I'm afraid, then you will really appreciate that when I wish all your players the best luck in the world, I really mean it!'

A stage performance of *The Paragon* by Cilfynydd and District Amateur Dramatic Society at the Workmen's Hall, Cilfynydd, on Wednesday 23 November 1960. President of the society was Councillor Roy Clayton, while L. Nidditch of the Ely Brewery Co. was their patron. *The Paragon* received excellent reviews in the local press and featured such local players as Richard Williams, Don Powell, Jean Jenkins, Bette Wilde, Mavis Caddy, Harry Morgan, Ron Cooper, Marion Rogers, John Roberts and Windsor Hobbs.

Sir Geraint Evans (1922-92) was born in William Street and was surrounded by music from birth. His father was a conductor and his mother, who died when he was a boy, was also a singer. The young Geraint was a talented pianist and violinist, and also sang in local productions. He left school at fourteen to work as a window dresser in a ladies clothes shop in Pontypridd. He carried on performing as an amateur until the outbreak of the Second World War. Geraint originally joined the RAF and became involved with the music department of the British Forces Network, performing regularly on the radio. The Austrian bass singer Theo Hermann heard him and gave him lessons. It was through Hermann's contacts that Geraint auditioned at the Royal Opera House, Covent Garden, on his return. He joined the company in 1947, and after starring in smaller roles he quickly progressed to perform Figaro when he was only twenty-six. Other character baritone roles soon followed, and with them increasing fame.

Sir Geraint Evans pictured in his most famous role as Verdi's *Falstaff*, which he sang in opera houses around the world, complete with 30lbs of foam padding! Other favourites included *Figaro, Beckmesser, Leporello* and *Dulcamara*. Another defining moment came in 1960 when he was asked to perform Figaro at La Scala in Milan, under the baton of the great Herbert von Karajan. He was the first British singer to have performed at La Scala in thirty-five years. In March 1964, he travelled to New York for another debut – this time at The Met, in a production of *Falstaff* directed by Zeffirelli. The conductor was Leonard Bernstein and the audience response was phenomenal. Vienna and Salzburg, San Francisco and Buenos Aires beckoned and Geraint became one of the very first international opera star jet-setters. He married Brenda, a schoolteacher who was also born in William Street, Cilfynydd. They lived mainly in London but in the 1960s they bought a holiday home in Aberaeron, where Sir Geraint could pursue one of his favourite pastimes – sailing. Geraint started to retire in 1982 – and during the extended period of farewell performances he was diagnosed as being diabetic. He continued to perform until around 1984 when he made his last appearance at Covent Garden in Donizetti's *L'Elisir D'Amore* but continued as a director of HTV Wales which he'd helped found in 1967. He also gave master classes and continued to sail his yacht *Y Marchog* (*The Knight*) and became high sheriff of Cardiganshire. When he died in 1992 hundreds of mourners lined the streets of Aberaeron to pay their respects to one of the world's great opera singers.

Opposite below: Stuart Burrows was born in William Street on 7 February 1933. He began his working career as a teacher but his magnificent talent as a tenor soon brought him enduring fame and good fortune. His recitals included works by Mozart, Beethoven, Berlioz, Schubert, Sullivan, Adams, Tippett, Tchaikovsky, Mallote, Mahler, Offenbach and Handel. He has earned worldwide recognition for being adept at oratorios, operas and specialising in the music of Puccini, Verdi, Donizetti and especially Mozart, earning him the title of The King of Mozart. In 1963, Stuart Burrows debuted in Cardiff with the Welsh National Opera as Ismael in Verdi's *Nabucco*. In 1967, his phenomenal performance during the Athens Festival brought him international acclaim. The well crafted version of Igor Stravinsky's *Oedipus Rex* was certain evidence of Stuart being one of the world's finest lyric tenors of all time. It was a performance requested by Stravinsky himself. He performed in *Don Giovanni* in Brussels; *Madam Butterfly* in Vienna; in Milan, he played in *Faust*; he performed both in *L'Elisir D'Amore* and the *Magic Flute* in San Francisco; *Die Entführung* at the Paris Opera; in Buenos Aires, he performed in *Tales of Hoffman* at the Theatre Cologne and at the Theatre de Le Monnaie, Belgium; the *Mozart Requiem* at the Cardiff Festival of Choirs in Wales; *Don Giovanni* at the San Diego Opera; and many times with the Royal Opera including roles in *Don Pasquale* and *La Sonambula*, and touring both Japan and the USA

Above: Beulah Baptist church girls' choir, *c.* 1955. This very successful chapel-based choir entertained audiences for many years. The conductor was Eva Paget and the accompanist was Rhoda Llewellyn.

Above: Howard Jones (1921-2004), from Howell Street. The son of David and Gladys Jones, he was the elder brother of Mostyn and Haydn. Howard was once judged by an international stage magazine to be the fifth most popular singer in the world. He started work as a trainee pit engineer at the Albion Colliery and saved the money for train fares so that he could take voice-training lessons in London. At the age of nineteen, while performing regularly in local dance bands, he was engaged by Stanley Black and the BBC Dance Band. He was later spotted by Joe Loss, then leader of one of Britain's top swing-bands, and was signed on at £55 a week. In his first year with the Loss Orchestra, he did fifty-two week-long tours, travelling to major theatres in Britain and the rest of Europe in the days when the music halls were still in business. He remained with Joe Loss for twelve years, appearing at the London Palladium. One of his records, *Jezebel*, sold a million copies. He settled in the Isle of Man when American bandleader, Woody Herman, asked Howard to join him to replace Frank Sinatra, but Howard declined. But the good times were coming to an end. Rock'n'Roll had arrived and the big bands fell out of fashion. Jobs were hard and following a divorce he met Marge, a girl from Leeds, who was making bookings at the one-time famous Buxton Hall Country Club at Rawdon. She booked Howard as an artiste, and the 'date' was to last for the next forty years when they married and moved to Steeton where Howard worked as an engineer.

Opposite: Stuart Burrows as Mozart's Don Giovanni. In New York Burrows has been accompanied by the talents of Sir Georg Solti, Zubin Mehta, Seiji Ozawa, Leonard Bernstein and Eugene Ormandy, among others, at the prestigious Carnegie Hall. He has also appeared in major roles at the Metropolitan Opera in New York City for more consecutive seasons than any British singer. He has collaborated with several other top flight orchestral organisations including the Academy of St Martin in the Fields, the Boston Symphony, the London Symphony and the Royal Philharmonic Orchestra. He has also had several professional performances in the rarified high altitudes of Santa Fe, New Mexico. Although well known for live and recorded performances, Stuart was no stranger to television. He has appeared on the small screen in Australia, North America and Europe, including a successful BBC television series called *Stuart Burrows Sings* which featured a variety of different periods and genres. The success of this musical review made it possible for more annual televised performances to follow. In 1981, he received an Honorary Doctorate from the University of Wales at Cardiff. A fellowship was awarded to him in 1989 from Trinity College, Carmarthen. The University of Wales at Aberystwyth presented him with an honorable fellowship in 1992.

Born in Mary Street on 7 June 1950, Gareth Wood was just twelve when he performed in clubs as a guitarist with pop band The Planets. He attended Pontypridd Grammar School and studied composition and the double bass at The Royal Academy of Music, joining the Royal Philharmonic Orchestra in 1972. Gareth has played for many of the world's greatest conductors, including Stokowski, Kempe, Karl Bohm, Haitink and Solti. He became Chairman of the Royal Philharmonic in 1991. As a composer, many works for bands followed and included test pieces for the 1977 Butlins Youth Band Contest, the 1980 New Zealand Brass Band championships and the 1992 European Championships. In 1981 his overture, *Suffolk Punch*, a commission by the Royal Philharmonic, was premiered in Ipswich where the work was encored. 1982 was the centenary of the famous Gunfight at the OK Corral and Gareth rearranged his overture, *Tombstone*, for the University of Arizona Symphonic Wind Band and it was played in the OK Corral. The National Youth Orchestra of Wales has also kept him busy, commissioning three sinfonettas and two fanfares. He has written for such occasions as the 150th anniversary of Cunard (performed onboard the *Queen Elizabeth II*), and the opening of the Kravis Centre in West Palm Beach, Florida. A fanfare overture was commissioned for the launch of the Cardiff Bay Development Corporation, as was Fantasy on Welsh Song which is performed every year at the last night of the Welsh Proms in Cardiff. He wrote a fanfare for the eightieth birthday of Yehudi Menuhin and has also written a violin concerto as a gift for Menuhin.

Fossicking, *c.* 1910. This practice shows the village's young men searching through the spoil on the tip in the hope of finding fossilised trees and ferns – a popular hobby since there were so many fossils found in the Albion Colliery while digging for coal.

Cilfynydd Hunters, 1926. Each chase was done on foot despite the dress code.

The Cilfynydd Strike Distress Parade. This picture was probably taken during the 1911 Cambrian dispute, where miners from other collieries assisted the striking colliers in the Rhondda by holding fundraising activities.

St John's Ambulance Association pictured in 1935 with the Dewar Shield which the Association won at the City Hall, Cardiff. They were also winners of the J.D. Morgan Cup in 1932, 1933 and 1934 and winners of the Dragon Shield in 1934. From left to right, back row: Melville Griffiths, Lewis Spear, Ken Pearce, Ron Pippin, Howard Thomas, Bryn Pearce, Vernon Williams, Patsy Ryan. Front row: Evan Perkins, Bill Edwards, B. Moore (undermanager at Albion Colliery), Fred Wells, Ken Crudge (Captain).

St John's Ambulance Brigade on an outing to Cardiff, *c.* 1950. From left to right, front row: Jean Clapham, Katherine Peck, Russell Dobbs, Mrs Dobbs, Lynette Williams, Marion Burton, Elvira Rees. Back row: Margaret Lloyd, Olive Burch, Betty Williams, Janette Mathews, Patricie Shead, Marjorie Jones. Every week Mrs Dobbs of Coedpenmaen and Miss Jenny (Janet) Burrows of William Street ran the local branch of St John's Ambulance.

Cilfynydd Scout Group following their camp at Newport, Pembrokeshire, in August 1958. The group was formed in September 1931 and met in the church hall. The officers were Mr A.F. Howell, Jack Cros, E.H. David, Percy Young, Luther Railton and W.J. Williams. Their first parade was on 25 October 1931 and later that month they attended a service at St Luke's church for the dedication of the legion standard. For a number of years they met in a prefabricated building that moved around the village several times before finally settling behind Bryn Road in 1946. In 1978 they moved to the former Unemployed Hall on Park Place, and Coun Emrys Peck was invited to open their new venue.

Cilfynydd Scouts' Christmas party, December 1959. The scouts held a Christmas concert in the hall before climbing aboard a lorry supplied by George Woolford and travelling around the village to sing carols.

A trip outside the Commercial Hotel, Cilfynydd Road, in 1915. Behind the vehicle is the entrance to the 360ft-long Coronation Bridge, erected in 1902. It bridged the Glamorganshire Canal and Albion Colliery Sidings to allow passengers access to the Cilfynydd Taff Vale railway station.

A charabanc trip organised by King's Garage of Cilfynydd Road. Garage owner Gerald King always claimed that his favourite trips were chapels or ladies' excursions because there was far less chance of drinking or fighting involved! Mr King is sat on the running board.

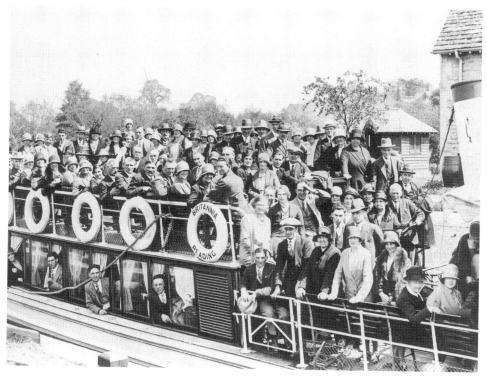

Cilfynydd residents on an outing to Windsor in 1925. The villagers are pictured on the River Thames as part of their daytrip. They travelled by special excursion train from Cilfynydd Station.

Cilfynydd residents on an outing to London, *c.* 1924. They travelled by train to the capital, before enjoying a charabanc trip around the popular sights. In this picture they are shown during their visit to the Houses of Parliament.

Residents on the steps of the Workmen's Hall, 1939. Many of these elderly inhabitants came to the village when it began to develop. They could vividly remember the disaster of 1894 and the tornado of 1913.

Members of Cilfynydd's first OAP Society met in the garden of Dundella. The get–together was to celebrate the 100th birthday of Mrs Williams (front centre) who had also received a message of congratulations from Buckingham Palace.

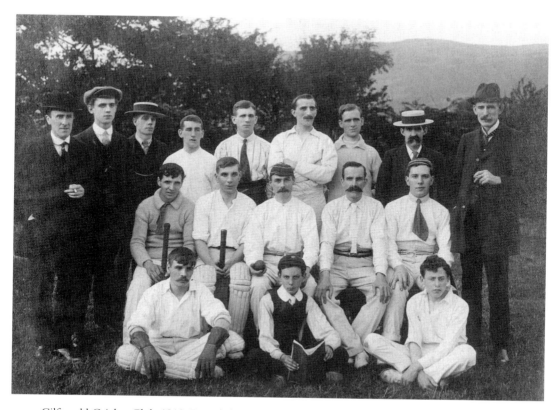

Cilfynydd Cricket Club, 1913. From left to right, back row: H. Cullen, E.G. Benson, R. Evans, T.D. James, A. Potter, B. Hughes, J. Davies (umpire). Middle row: P.J. Jones (president), E. Lewis, G. Wride, J. Jones (captain), S. Matthews, J. Leonard, H.H. Evans (vice president). Front row: J. Wood, S. Hopkins, J. Evans.

Cilfynydd Juniors Athletic Football Club, who remained unbeaten for the entire 1919/20 season. From left to right, back row: J. Williams (trainer), R. Coles (treasurer), W. Manning, D. Isaac, W. Barrett, T. Isaac, L. Jenkins, T. Williams (trainer). Middle row: H. Lusimope, W. Davies, T. Knight (captain) E.E. Talbot (playing secretary), I. Evans (vice captain). Front row: G. Williams, E. Thomas (mascot) and D.J. Williams.

Cilfynydd Welfare AFC and committee, 1952/53 season. Members of the South Wales Amateur League Division One, they were winners of the South Wales and Monmouth Amateur Cup in the 1951/52 season and runners-up in the 1952/53 season. The team were also the winners of the 1951, 1952, 1953 and 1954 Greyhound Cup. In 1972 they were runners-up in the Corinthian Cup finals. Their headquarters was the Cilfynydd Inn and they played on the recreation ground with the colours of amber, black trimmed and black shorts. The president was Tony Carini, standing third from the right.

Cilfynydd Welfare AFC, 1952/53 season, winners of the South Wales and Monmouth Cup final. From left to right, back row: –?–, Elwyn Morgan, Johnny Lott, Roy Boulton, Eric Hopkins. Front row: Stuart Burrows, –?–, Archie Davies, Charlie Morgan, Don Serpel, David Evans. Stuart Burrows was one of a few local sportsmen invited to controversially 'go north' and play for rugby league. Newly married and a schoolteacher, he was surprised at the age of twenty-four to receive such an invitation. He even went so far as to walk onto Cardiff railway station with a ticket in his hand for the journey, but at the last minute he didn't travel. If he had, then the world may well have been robbed of one of its finest lyric tenors.

Cilfynydd Welfare AFC, c. 1955. A stalwart of the team for almost sixty years was Bert Weston who had been presented with tickets for the FA Cup as a gift from the club for his dedicated service. Sadly, he died just days prior to the game.

Cilfynydd Athletic Football Club, 1968/69 season. From left to right, back row: Ike Davies, Evan Hassell, Tudor Griffiths, Johnny Lock, Terry Davey, Alan Edwards, Glyn Price, Gerwyn Caffrey, David Jones, Burt Weston. Front row: Tony Ross, -?-, Bruce Evans (Captain), Arwel Davies, Mike Jones, Brian Haggert.

Opposite above, left: Alf Gibbs. The Gibbs family were well known for their sporting exploits, particularly in the fields of weightlifting and boxing. Alf excelled himself at both, along with rugby and running and was even the South Wales roller skating champion. His brothers Ben, Arthur, Dick and Will were all competent sportsmen. Their sister, Laura, became a British weightlifting champion. Their parents, George and Jane Gibbs, came to Cilfynydd from Weymouth. George was a keen cricketer and a leading runner in his day. His children would travel around the South Wales workmen's halls and lift weights as a family team. Will could make a single-handed lift of 175lbs. Arthur was the boxer, while Alf boxed at bantamweight but his appearances were mainly restricted to fairground booths. Dick fought the famous Peter Jackson during his career. Alf and Arthur also won the Pontypridd Powderhall Sprinting Championships over 100 yards on a cinder track at Taff Vale Park. The family also made a name for themselves as a musical act, with 'Come and See Atlas and Vulcana' proclaimed on the posters. Laura would sing while the brothers lifted weights until Laura herself lifted the weights while bursting into song. During the First World War, Alf served in the trenches in France before returning to marry Gertrude Evans and work in the Albion Colliery. During the depression of the 1930s he became a car mechanic to motorbike rider Tal Lougher. He later worked for BOAC before retiring in 1963.

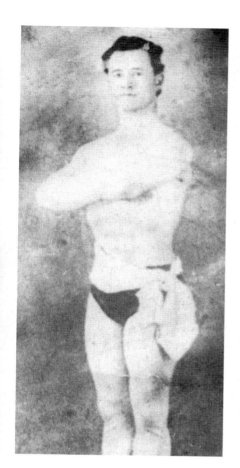

Above right: Dai Dower MBE. The brilliant former flyweight champion was born on 20 June 1933 in Abercynon and grew up to become a national hero. Along with his father, also named David, they ran the Richard's Hotel between 1954 and 1958. Dai had a specially made boxing ring built at the back of the building for the locals to watch him train. When they moved into the pub they were selling a barrel a week, within months it was fifteen. He was quick, elusive and fast punching, with a personality to match his talents. In 1952 he represented Britain at the Olympic Games as an amateur. His championship contests kept the nation glued to the wireless. In October 1954, he produced a fantastic display of boxing skills to beat the Zulu flyweight, Jake Tuli, for the Empire title. The following February he took the British title from Eric Marsden over fifteen dazzling rounds. A month later he made it a hat-trick by snatching the European title with a points win against Italy's Nazzareno Gravielli. Dai's European title went when he was knocked out by Young Martin of Spain in the twelfth round. It was a brutal fight – twelve times the Welshman was knocked off his feet, twelve times he got back up, despite a broken rib. Even more painful was his world title defeat at the fists of Argentina's Pascual Perez. At twenty-five, the former PTI in the army hung up his gloves and became the sports manager at Ringwood Grammar School (later Bournemouth University) and retired at sixty-five. In 1998 he was awarded the MBE from the Queen at Buckingham Palace and received an honorary degree from Bournemouth University.

Cilfynydd Inn B Darts Team, Whitbread League B. Section winners in 1975. From left to right, back row: Ron Philips, Wyn Fort, Michael Baker, Alun Evans, Ron Jones, Alan Walters. Front row: Howell Griffiths, William Bowen (captain), Arwel Davies.

Cilfynydd Ladies' Soccer team pictured with their trainers S. Davies and R. Jones, with Councillor Clayton. From left to right, back row: M. Cotter, G. Jones, O. Burch. Middle row: B. Cox, D. Hughes, P. Byard, M. Penny. Front row: G. Edwards, E. Jones, N. Smith (captain).

Right: Joe Jones of Mary Street, *c.* 1935. A well-known rugby player, he played for Cilfynydd RFC but eventually played rugby league in Wigan and Barrow. For a short while he returned to the village and played football because the local rugby club would not allow him to play since he'd 'gone north'. He was one of several players to take the leap to rugby league, including Stan Cornelius, Arthur Peck and Iorrie Isaac.

Opposite below: A group of players at the Billiard Hall. Pictured with the players is well-known councillor Emrys Peck. The hall, a wooden structure, was destroyed by a fire in 1981. It was a great loss to village life because it had been a firm favourite with local sportsmen over many years.

Glyn Davies of William Street. He made many appearances as outside-half for Wales between 1946 and 1953. Glyn, whose sister Brenda married Geraint Evans, was selected to play for Wales in the 1946 Victory International, alongside his Pontypridd half-back partner Wynford Davies, while they were still attending the local grammar school. Glyn went on to win eleven caps for his country. He was recognised as a mercurial outside-half, a beautiful runner with a devastating sidestep, and was nicknamed 'El Supremo' by his adoring fans. He went on to captain Cambridge University, and later played for Bristol, Newport and Glamorgan Wanderers. In a lasting tribute, writer Alun Richards said of Glyn Davies, 'On his day – the Matador – His Excellency – El Supremo – the most graceful and elegant of them all'.

Cilfynydd United XV team, 1908/09 season. The team remained undefeated throughout the entire season. The captain was T.J. Rees, with W.J. Rosser as president and A. Seymour as secretary. The origins of the team are believed to coincide with the sinking of the Albion Colliery. Experiencing mixed fortunes in the early years, the club finally enjoyed three unbeaten seasons prior to the outbreak of the First World War and winning the Rhondda League.

Above left: Cilfynydd XV Rugby Team, 1925/26 season. Four Cilfynydd players featured in the Mid-District side that played against the New Zealand All Blacks in the 1936/37 season. This period saw further success for the club, with four Glamorgan league championships and, also, four Glamorgan KO Cup wins. The successful period heralded the emergence of the three Welsh internationals. The village club has produced Iorrie Isaacs, Maldwyn James and Glyn Davies.

Above right: Iorwerth Isaac (1910-66). Born in Cilfynydd on 4 October 1910, Iori attended the Intermediate County School for Boys, Pontypridd, and was captain of the school rugby team. He obtained his international cap for the Welsh secondary schools against France at Cardiff and later went on to enjoy an illustrious career in both rugby league and union. In September 1929 he joined the Glamorgan County Constabulary and served in Cardiff, during which time he played rugby for Cardiff Rugby Club and Welsh and British Police XVs. On 4 August 1933, having played twice for Wales, he resigned from the police force after being offered professional status by Leeds Rugby Football Club, and the opportunity to train as a teacher at Headingly College. He attended Leeds City Training College between 1933 and 1935 as a trainee teacher. In 1936 he joined the staff of Shadwell Intermediate School and three years later was principal teacher at the opening of Druid's Heath School, Aldridge, by Dr Barnardo's. During the war he saw service in the RAF but rejoined Druid's Heath in 1946 and in 1947 was appointed headmaster of Quinta School, Oswestry, where he served until his sudden death. In 1933, Iori toured France with Leeds to pioneer rugby league, playing at Paris Lyons and Villeneuve. In 1936, Leeds travelled to London for their first appearance at the new Empire Stadium at Wembley for the Rugby League Cup. Before a record crowd of 51,000, Leeds equalled Huddersfield's record for cup wins with their fourth, via an 18-2 win over Warrington in a disappointing final. Iori gave Leeds the lead when after seven minutes he took the ball in his stride to dive straight for the touch, just wide of the posts. During his time at Leeds Iori made eighty-three appearances, and scored eighteen tries. He again obtained a Welsh International cap at Twickenham when they laid the 'bogey' against England on 21 January 1933. Wales had waited twenty-three years for it and this first success was watched by a record championship-match attendance of 64,000, which included the Prince of Wales. He represented Wales again at Murrayfield on 4 February 1933 when he played against Scotland as flanker. In the same year he played for Great Britain in league football against France – the only Welshman so far to get caps in both codes of the game in the same season. He died on 15 April 1966 at Wrexham, aged fifty-five.

Cilfynydd XV Rugby Team, 1935/36 season. From left to right, front row: Jackie James, Jacke Rowe, Maldwyn James. Second row: Verdun Lloyd, Tudor Burton, Bray Lewis, Stan Cornelius, Eifion Williams, Iori Jones. Third row: George Holland, -?-, Mr Hawkins, Don Players, Tom Goodwin, Ted Yorath, Bill Jones, Don Jones, W. Hughes, Tom James, Dai Matthes, W. Crudge (trainer). Back row: Walter Real, Edwin Snooks, W. James, Joe Owen, Stan Lawton, Will Amos, Gwyn Jones, Ron Penny, -?-, -?-.

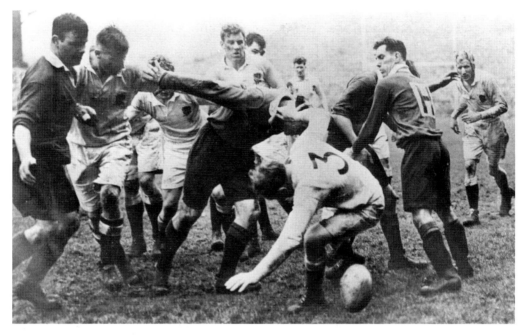

David Maldwyn James (1913-2003) pictured on the right, during the Wales vs England game at Twickenham in 1948. Born in Mary Street on 28 June 1913, Maldwyn James became one of a select band of players who experienced first-class rugby before and after the Second World War. He attended Pontypridd Grammar School and played for the Cilfynydd and Pontypridd clubs, and ten times for Glamorgan County. Between 1937 and 1938 he was selected for the Welsh international trials but a serious injury to his right foot kept him out of the game until 1941. In 1945 he joined Cardiff and was an immediate success. Blessed with all the skills, including goal-kicking, he contributed 145 points during the season and played in four 'Victory' internationals for Wales. Caps were not awarded for the latter, but he won full honours two years later. At thirty-four he became the third oldest player to make his debut for Wales. That was against Australia and he completed a winning double having already helped the Cardiff side to beat the Wallabies. He played throughout the 1948 international season and then hung up his boots to concentrate on a successful mining career. Maldwyn James was a qualified in 1944 and for many years worked at the Albion Colliery. He was also a prominent official of the National Coal Board in the South Wales area. In 1952 he became president of the Tylorstown club and after that served on the Cardiff Rugby Club committee and eventually as club chairman. He died on 19 July 2003 at the age of ninety.

Cilfynydd XV Rugby Team, 1938/39 season. The 'Black and Ambers' were winners of the Glamorgan League for four consecutive seasons since 1934, and winners of the Glamorgan League Knockout Cup for five consecutive seasons from 1933. From left to right, back row: Jack Osbourne (trainer), Tony Bowsher, Rupert Cummings, Stan Pruett, V. Harvey, William Perry, J. Jeffries, R. Hopkins, A. Lewis, Tom James, Tom Smith, H. Davies. Middle row: J. Jackles, T. Evans (chairman), G. Ashman, A. Cornelius (captain), J.W. Jordan (president), J. Price, Maldwyn James. W.H. Jones (secretary), A.T. Locke (treasurer). Front row: Joe Owen, T. Davies, Emrys Peck, Alby Harris. D. Jenkins, Ruben King.

Players pictured with the young Dudley Lloyd, later to become president of Cilfynydd RFC. From left to right: Alwyn Morgan, David Williams, Glyn Davies, Joe Smith, Phillip Lewis and Len Jones.

Cilfynydd XV Rugby Team, 1959/60 season. From left to right, standing: E. Lloyd, S. Smith, G. Lloyd, D. Lewis, T. Lloyd, J.H. Jones, G. Taverner, –?–, –?–, P. Lewis. Seated: –?–, G. Hamer, L. Jones, J. Smith, T. Ryan, –?–, B. Griffiths.

Cilfynydd XV Rugby Team, 1953/54 season. During the following season they won the Mid-District Championship and the success was repeated in the 1956/57 season when they won the Mid-District Cup.

Cilfynydd Rugby Club Committee, c. 1960. From left to right, back row: G. Jones, O. Fletcher, T. Rees, G. Gough, B. Matthews, W. Jacobs, J. Morgan, R. Bennett, C. Penny. Front row: E. Loyd, R. Cooper, J. Williams, H. Butler, G. Davies, R. Penny, G. Hamer.

Members laying the foundation of the present Cilfynydd Rugby Clubhouse, 1966. This is the site of the former Cwm Cottages, probably the earliest dwellings in the original village of Ynyscaedudwg In 1974, the club lost in the semi-final of the Glamorgan Silver Ball, and again suffered the same fate the following season.

Cilfynydd XV Rugby Team, 1978/79 season. The 1980/81 season saw the club win the Mid-District Club and also a seven-a-side tournament at Drybrook RFC, in Gloucester. The success continued in 1981 when the Harlequins won the Tom Coleman Cup. In 1983, the club enjoyed the best season ever, setting up a record total for a season with 1,033 points and the club was also runner-up in six leading competitions. Included in this success was the Silver Ball and the Presidents' Cup. The 1984/85 season saw them finish runners-up in the Coleman Cup and, in the following season, the club was runner-up in the Mid-District Cup and won the Glamorgan County Ushers Trophy for the most tries. In 1993, the club enjoyed a successful tour of Canada – coming home unbeaten.

Cilfynydd, 2006. The author would like to thank all those who have given their assistance to
the completion of this publication, namely: Hywel Matthews and Edwina Smart at Pontypridd
Library, all at Pontypridd Museum, John Lewis, David Male, Susan Meyrick, Andrew Jones, Mrs
Barrington, Gillian Lloyd, Gareth Bowen, Cilfynydd RFC, Steve King, Patricia Jones, Nigel Jones,
John Roberts, Arwel Davies, Alan Rochford, Helen Langdon, Ruby Morgan, Rhianwen Cooper,
Mario Carini, Alun Byrnes, David Male, Gaynor and Keith Bennett, Jean Bennett, Hayden Jones,
Gethyn Rees, Elvira Scammel, Peter Morgan, Mrs J. Thomas, Julie Morgan, Gwyn Hockin, Terry

Blackman, Mary Fletcher, Stuart Burrows, May Gulliford, Howard Paget, Mal Adams, David Isaac, Maria Gee, Pat Ryan, Glenys Rees, Dai Dower, Lady Brenda Evans and John Burrows. He would also like to pay particular tribute to Alun Caffrey, Jessica Evans and Stuart Evans for their interest in the publication. Above all, he would like to thank Meurig Evans for his tireless work in editing the project and for so freely giving his time, dedication and archive material which has undoubtedly enhanced the publication by a tremendous degree.

Other local titles published by Tempus

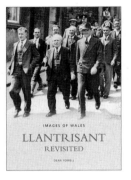

Pontypridd: A Market Town
DEAN POWELL

Compiled with 200 images, this selection highlights some of the changes and events that have taken place in the South Wales market town of Pontypridd. From glimpses of heavy industry, including the Ynysangharad Works and surrounding collieries, to the arrival of the first electric tram to Pontypridd in March 1905, all aspects of working and social life are chronicled here. Aspects of everyday life are also recalled, from shops and pubs, places of worship and public buildings, to celebrations and local sporting heroes.

0 7524 3578 7

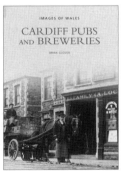

Llantrisant Revisited
DEAN POWELLR

This fascinating collection of over 200 old images pays tribute to the people who have proudly called Llantrisant their home. Commanding an outstanding setting on the crest of a hill, Llantrisant's splendour lies in its enchanting beauty and celebrated past. Bloodthirsty battles, pioneering acts of cremation and captured kings of England have all played a part in shaping the town, as have the generations of families who have lived here.

0 7524 3216 X

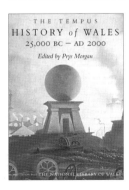

Cardiff Pubs and Breweries
BRIAN GLOVER

Illustrated with over 100 old photographs, postcards and promotional advertisements, *Cardiff Pubs and Breweries* looks at the beers and breweries which vanished and the one which survived. Glimpses of working and social life, and some of the pubs' more lively clientele – those who found themselves 'drinking in the dark' – are also featured, each image recalling the fascinating social history of Cardiff's brewing industry.

0 7524 3110 2

The Tempus History of Wales
PRYS MORGAN

Wales was at the heart of the Industrial Revolution, with towns like Merthyr Tydfil driving the engine of the British Empire. The cultural and social divide between modern, industrialised Wales and the traditional agricultural areas is explored within this comprehensive volume.

0 7524 1983 8

If you are interested in purchasing other books published by Tempus, or in case you have difficulty finding any Tempus books in your local bookshop, you can also place orders directly through our website

www.tempus-publishing.com